高等职业教育旅游类专业新形态教材

酒店服务英语
Hotel Service English

主 编 金 郁 韩 婷 万豫晨

北京理工大学出版社
BEIJING INSTITUTE OF TECHNOLOGY PRESS

内 容 提 要

酒店服务英语是酒店管理与数字化运营专业的核心课程，通过学习本课程，学生可以了解酒店行业特点，认识高星级酒店主要前线部门的各个岗位，掌握不同岗位所需的专业知识和职业技能。本书以酒店管理与数字化运营专业人才培养目标为依据，以高星级酒店主要服务性工作岗位为基础，详细介绍了高星级酒店核心岗位的服务流程，并融入了邮轮运营服务岗位的能力要求。本书设置了5个项目、20个学习任务，任务工单包含理论测试和技能操作，集教材、学习笔记、作业与考核评价于一体，是校企合作创新实践的专业教材。

本书可作为高等院校酒店管理与数字化运营专业教学用书，也可以作为星级酒店员工培训教材，还可作为邮轮运营服务1+X证书考试学习用书。

版权专有　侵权必究

图书在版编目（CIP）数据

酒店服务英语 / 金郁，韩婷，万豫晨主编.--北京：
北京理工大学出版社，2021.9
　　ISBN 978-7-5763-0380-3

Ⅰ.①酒…　Ⅱ.①金…②韩…③万…　Ⅲ.①饭店－商业服务－英语－高等职业教育－教材　Ⅳ.①F719.2

中国版本图书馆CIP数据核字（2021）第191333号

出版发行 / 北京理工大学出版社有限责任公司
社　　址 / 北京市海淀区中关村南大街5号
邮　　编 / 100081
电　　话 /（010）68914775（总编室）
　　　　　（010）82562903（教材售后服务热线）
　　　　　（010）68944723（其他图书服务热线）
网　　址 / http://www.bitpress.com.cn
经　　销 / 全国各地新华书店
印　　刷 / 河北鑫彩博图印刷有限公司
开　　本 / 787毫米×1092毫米　1/16
印　　张 / 13　　　　　　　　　　　　　　　　责任编辑 / 阎少华
字　　数 / 293千字　　　　　　　　　　　　　　文案编辑 / 阎少华
版　　次 / 2021年9月第1版　2021年9月第1次印刷　责任校对 / 周瑞红
定　　价 / 48.00元　　　　　　　　　　　　　　责任印制 / 边心超

图书出现印装质量问题，请拨打售后服务热线，本社负责调换

前 言

酒店服务英语作为酒店管理与数字化运营专业的核心课程，旨在培养高星级酒店、国际邮轮及相关行业中运用英语服务的高技能型人才。本书为辽宁建筑职业学院旅游管理学院与沈阳丽都索菲特酒店深度校企合作编写的教材，紧跟产业发展趋势和行业人才需求，及时将产业发展的新技术、新工艺、新规范纳入教材，反映典型岗位（群）职业能力要求，集教材、教学资源、学习笔记、作业于一体。同时，将劳动精神、审美教育等元素有机融入教学设计，以实现"立德树人"的人才培养总体目标。

本书由辽宁建筑职业学院金郁、韩婷及沈阳丽都索菲特酒店培训经理万豫晨担任主编。具体编写分工为：韩婷编写项目1、项目2及相应工单，金郁编写项目3、项目4、项目5及相应工单，万豫晨负责本书审定工作。

本书在编写过程中，引用了部分网络资源及相关专业的教材，在此一并致以诚挚的谢意。

由于编者水平有限，如有疏漏或不足之处，恳请广大读者批评指正。

编　者

目 录

项目 1 The Front Office（前厅部） ················· 1

学习任务 1 Room Reservation（客房预订服务）················· 1
学习任务 2 Check In（入住登记服务）················· 10
学习任务 3 Exchanging Foreign Currency（外币兑换服务）················· 19
学习任务 4 Check Out（结账退宿服务）················· 24

项目 2 The Housekeeping（客房部） ················· 40

学习任务 1 Introducing Facilities（介绍酒店设施与服务）················· 40
学习任务 2 Room Cleaning Service（客房清扫服务）················· 47
学习任务 3 Laundry Service（洗衣服务）················· 55
学习任务 4 Ordering Room Service（客房订餐服务）················· 62
学习任务 5 Delivering Room Service（客房送餐服务）················· 71

项目 3 The Food & Beverage（餐饮部） ················· 89

学习任务 1 Booking a Table（预订餐台服务）················· 89
学习任务 2 Leading the Guest（引客入位服务）················· 98
学习任务 3 Serving Chinese Food（中餐服务）················· 102
学习任务 4 Serving Western Food（西餐服务）················· 107
学习任务 5 Bar Service（酒吧服务）················· 112
学习任务 6 Paying the Bill（餐厅结账服务）················· 116
学习任务 7 Handling Complaints（处理投诉）················· 120

项目 4　The Fitness Center（康乐部） ··· 137

学习任务 1　Gym Service（健身房服务） ··· 137

学习任务 2　Swimming and Bowling Service（泳池及保龄球服务） ············· 144

项目 5　The Business Center（商务中心） ·· 152

学习任务 1　Booking Tickets（票务服务） ·· 152

学习任务 2　Secretarial Service（文秘服务） ·· 156

任务工单 ·· 165

The Front Office(前厅部)

学习任务1 Room Reservation(客房预订服务)

工作任务	Room Reservation (客房预订服务)	教学模式	线上线下混合教学模式 情境模拟教学模式
建议学时	4学时	教学地点	智慧教室或多媒体教室
任务描述	美国TJ电子公司的Tom Hanks先生等一行七人定于8月2日至8月10日到沈阳参加东北亚贸易洽谈会,决定入住沈阳丽都索菲特酒店(Sofitel Shenyang Lido Hotel),他们通过电话预订的方式预订了房间,解决在沈阳停留期间的住宿问题,他的助手Grace Miller打电话给沈阳丽都索菲特酒店预订一些客房		
学习目标	1. 掌握客房预订相关的英文词汇及各种房间类型的英文表达。 2. 掌握客房预订的服务程序及各个程序的英文表达。 3. 能用英文处理客房预订,取消和更改预订服务。 4. 当客房订满时,能用英文向客人提出解决方案。 5. 培养敬业严谨的工作作风和爱岗敬业的品德。 6. 树立正确的酒店职业观和价值观		

头脑风暴

1. 如果你是预订员，如何受理 Miller 女士的预订？服务程序是什么？需要从 Miller 女士那里获知哪些信息？
2. 如果客人行程有变，需要更改住宿时间或取消预订，需如何处理？
3. 如果没有合适的房间或预订已满，如何解决？

词汇储备

词汇 Vocabulary

1. reserve (book)　　v. 预订　　reservation　　n. 预订
2. room reservation　　客房预订
3. arrival date　　到店日期
4. departure date　　离店日期
5. special request　　特殊需求
6. personal information　　个人信息
7. room available　　空房
8. room rate /daily rate　　房价
9. recommend　　v. 推荐　　recommendation　　n. 推荐
10. confirm　　v. 确认　　confirmation　　n. 确认
11. cancel　　v. 取消　　cancellation　　n. 取消

房型 Room Type

1. 单人间　　single room
2. 大床房　　double room
3. 标准间　　standard room / twin room
4. 三人间　　triple room
5. 套房　　suite
6. 家庭套房　　family suite
7. 商务套房　　business suite
8. 豪华套房　　deluxe suite
9. 复式套房　　duplex suite
10. 总统套房　　presidential suite
11. 相邻房　　adjoining rooms
12. 连通房　　connecting rooms

服务流程

客房预订服务流程如下：

1. Greetings.
   问候。

受理预订

2. Asking the guest the reservation information.

   询问客人预订信息。

   （1）room type.

   客人所需房型。

   （2）arrival date and time for staying.

   到店日期及停留时间。

   （3）number of persons.

   客人数量。

   （4）special requests.

   特殊需求。

3. Checking (the information in the computer).

   核对预订记录。

4. Asking the guest the personal information.

   询问客人个人信息。

5. Confirming reservation.

   确认信息。

6. Expressing the wishes.

   表达祝愿。

情境模拟

1. The first step: Greetings.

   第一步：问候。常用的句子有：

   a. Room reservations. May I help you?

   预订部，您有什么需要吗？

   b. Good morning, sir/ madam. Room reservations, what can I do for you?

   早上好，女士/先生。预订部，有什么能帮到您的？

   c. Hilton hotel. Reservations, (how) may I help you?

   希尔顿酒店，预订部，有什么能帮到您的？

   d. Sofitel Hotel. (This is) Tina speaking. What can I do for you?（电话）

   索菲特酒店。我是 Tina。有什么能帮到您的？

情境 1：Miller 女士通过打电话的方式，想要预订索菲特酒店的房间。

Sofitel Hotel. Reservations, may I help you?

情境 2：下午，一位男士来到前台想要预订客房。

Good afternoon, sir. How may I help you?

情境 3：预订部的 Jane 晚上接到一位女士的订房电话。

Good evening, this is Jane speaking. May I help you?

2. The second step: Asking the guest the reservation information.
   第二步：询问客人预订信息。
   （1）room type.
   　　客人所需房型。
   （2）arrival date and time for staying.
   　　到店日期及停留时间。
   （3）number of persons.
   　　客人数量。
   （4）special requests.
   　　特殊需求。

询问客人所需房型，常用的句子有：
   a. What kind/sort of room would you like, sir/madam?
      先生/女士，您想要哪种房型？
   b. What kind/sort of room would you prefer, sir/madam?
      先生/女士，您想要哪种房型？
   c. A double room or a standard room?
      一个双人间（大床间）还是一个标准间？

情境 1：询问 Miller 女士想要预订索菲特酒店的哪种房间。
   What kind of room would you like, madam?

情境 2：一位男士来到前台，想要预订客房。
   What sort of room would you prefer, sir? A single room or a double room?

询问客人的到店日期及停留时间。
   a. For which date (s), sir?
      您从哪天开始入住？
   b. How many nights (will you be staying)?
      您一共住几晚？
   c. From which date and for how many nights?
      您从哪天开始入住，共住几晚？
   d. Your arrival and departure dates?
      您的到店日期和离店日期？
   e. When would you like it (your room), sir?
      您什么时候开始入住？

情境 1：Miller 女士想要在她们团队到沈阳工作期间预订几天的客房（电话）。
   From which date and for how many nights, madam?

情境 2：询问一位男性客人想要住几晚。

  How many nights, sir?

询问客人的数量及有无特殊需求。

 a. For how many persons/people?
  一共多少人？

 b. How many persons are there in your party?
  一行共多少人？

 c. Do you have any special requests with your room?
  您对房间有什么特殊需求吗？

 d. Any special requests with your room, sir?
  先生，您对房间有什么特殊需求吗？

情境 1：Miller 女士电话预订房间，询问其人数。

  For how many persons/people, madam?

情境 2：住店客人 Smith 先生想要给他的朋友订一个单人间，询问其有无特殊需求。

  Mr. Smith, do you have any special requests with the room?

3. The third step: Checking (the information in the computer).
  第三步：核对预订记录。常用的句子有：

 a. Just a moment/minute, please. I will check it.

 b. Hold on, please. I will check the room availability.（电话）

 c. Please hold the line.（电话）

 d. Would you mind waiting a moment?

情境 1：让电话预订的 Miller 女士稍等一会儿。

  Hold on, please, madam. I will check the room availability.

情境 2：让当面预订的住店客人 Smith 先生稍等一会儿。

  Just a minute, please, Mr. Smith. I will check it.

4. The fourth step: Asking the guest the personal information.
  第四步：询问客人个人信息。常用的句子有：

 a. May I have your name and telephone number?
  请问您的名字和电话是……？

 b. May I know your name and contact number?
  请问您的名字和联系电话是……？

 c. May I know your room number?
  请问您的房号是……？

情境 1：询问住店客人 Smith 先生的联系方式和房号。

Mr. Smith, may I know your contact number and room number, please?

情境 2：通过电话询问女性客人的个人信息。

May I have your name and telephone number, madam?

5. The fifth step: Confirming reservation

   第五步：确认预订信息。常用的句子有：

   a. Sir, I'd like to confirm your reservation…Am I right?

   先生，我确认一下您的预订信息……对吗？

   b. Let me confirm your reservation…Is that correct?

   我确认一下您的预订信息……对吗？

   c. So, Mr.Smith, you have booked…Is that right?

   Smith 先生，您预订了……对吗？

情境 1：住店客人 Smith 先生为他的朋友预订了一个三晚的单人间，日期为 5 月 2 日到 5 月 4 日晚，和 Smith 先生当面确认一下预订信息。

So, Mr.Smith, you have booked a single room for three nights from May, 2nd to 4th, and your telephone number is 13698356219. Is that right?

情境 2：Miller 女士通过电话为其团队成员预订了三间商务套房和一间豪华套房预订七晚，如何与客人确认预订信息。

Madam, I'd like to confirm your reservation, you booked three business suites and a deluxe suite for seven nights. Am I right?

情境 3：一位男士电话预订一间家庭套房，要求房间朝阳并为其女儿准备一个生日蛋糕，如何与客人确认预订信息。

Sir, let me confirm your reservation, you reserved a family suite for your family, and the room needs to face the south and a birthday cake is needed for your daughter. Is that correct?

6. The sixth step: Expressing the wishes.

   第六步：表达祝愿。常用的句子有：

   a. We look forward to serving you.

   期待着为您服务。

   b. We are expecting to have you here.

   期待着在酒店见到您。

   c. Thank you for your reservation.We look forward to your arrival.

   感谢您的预订。期待着您的光临。

情境 1： 住店客人 Smith 先生预订完成，与 Smith 先生道别。

Mr. Smith, We look forward to serving you.

情境 2： Miller 女士电话预订完餐位，与客人道别。

Thank you for your reservation. We look forward to your arrival.

能力进阶

取消预订服务

客人行程有变，需要取消或更改预订，服务程序及常用的句子有：

1. The first step: Greetings.

   第一步：问候。

2. The second step: Asking the guest's name or the way of the reservation.

   第二步：询问客人是以谁的名字预订的或询问客人是以何种方式预订的。常用的句子有：

   a. In whose name was the reservation made?
      您是以谁的名字预订的？

   b. In what way was the reservation made?
      您是以何种方式预订的？

   c. Was the reservation made in John Smith?
      您是以 John Smith 先生的名字预订的吗？

   d. What was the date of the reservation?
      您是哪天预订的？

3. The third step: Checking (the information in the computer).

   第三步：核对预订记录。

4. The fourth step: Asking the guest's request.

   第四步：询问客人（新的）需求。常用的句子有：

   a. How would you like to change/revise?
      您想如何更改？

   b. How would you like to change your previous reservation?
      您想如何更改您之前的预订？

   c. How to change please, sir?
      先生，您想如何更改？

   d. Would you like to extend your reservation for two more nights?
      你想把预订再延长两晚吗？

5. The fifth step: Confirming reservation.

   第五步：确认信息。常用的句子有：

a. I will change/cancel/extend/ your reservation for you.

我将为您更改 / 取消 / 延长您的预订。

b. Mr. Smith, I will cancel your reservation for July, 5th for three nights. My name is Tina. Glad to be of your service.

Smith 先生，我为您取消 7 月 5 号起三晚的预订。我是 Tina，很高兴为您服务。

6. The sixth step: Expressing the wishes.

第六步：表达祝愿。常用的句子有：

a. We look forward to another chance to serve you.（针对取消预订）

我们期待着再有机会为您服务。

b. We look forward to having another opportunity to serve you.（针对取消预订）

我们期待着再有机会为您服务。

当酒店客房预订已满时，常用的句子有：

a. I'm sorry, but we are fully booked on that date.

很抱歉，我们那天的客房预订已满。

b. All of our rooms are fully booked/occupied. We're very sorry, sir. We hope you could understand us.

很抱歉先生，我们所有的客房预订已满，希望得到您的理解。

c. Sir, how about a single room, the suites are fully booked now.

先生，单人间怎么样？套房现在预订已满。

d. We don't have any family suites available. Would you mind a deluxe suite instead?

我们没有家庭套房了，您看豪华套房行吗？

e. It's a pity there are not any vacant rooms then. Would you mind changing the reservation date?

太遗憾了，那天我们没有空房了。您能否把预订日期更改一下呢？

f. Sir, if you like, I would like to suggest another hotel which is near ours.

先生，如果您不介意，我为您推荐离我们距离很近的其他酒店行吗？

语言使用

"SERVICE"这个单词对于酒店人的真正含义

S 即 Smile（微笑），要给每一位客人提供微笑服务。

E 即 Excellent（出色），要将每一项小的服务工作都做得很好。

R 即 Ready（准备好），要随时准备好为客人服务。

V 即 Viewing（看待），要把每一位客人都看作需要给予特殊照顾的贵宾。

I 即 Inviting（邀请），在每一次服务结束时，都要邀请客人再次光临。

C 即 Creation（创造），要精心创造出使客人能享受其热情服务的气氛。

E 即 Eye（眼光），要用热情好客的眼光关注客人，预判客人的需求，并及时为其提供服务，使客人时刻感受到关心。

项目 1　The Front Office（前厅部）

能力训练

情境 1：

美国 TJ 电子公司的 Hanks 先生等一行七人定于 8 月 2 日至 8 月 10 日到沈阳参加东北亚贸易洽谈会，决定入住沈阳丽都索菲特酒店，他们通过电话预订的方式预订了三间商务套房和一间豪华套房，解决在沈阳停留期间的住宿问题。

Grace Miller, Hanks' assistant（助理）, calls to Sofitel Shenyang Lido Hotel, she would like to book some rooms...

要求：两人一组，完成对话。

情境 2：

Hanks 先生一行人之前预订了沈阳丽都索菲特酒店的套房，原定于 8 月 10 离开沈阳返回洛杉矶，但临时改变了行程，因还要参加另一个重要会议，所以决定多住两天。

要求：两人一组，完成对话。

学习任务 2　Check In（入住登记服务）

工作任务	Check In（入住登记服务）	教学模式	线上线下混合教学模式 情境模拟教学模式
建议学时	4 学时	教学地点	智慧教室或多媒体教室
任务描述	Hanks 先生等一行 7 人如期到达沈阳，来到沈阳丽都索菲特酒店。刚进大堂，接待员接待了他们并为他们办理入住登记手续		
学习目标	1. 掌握客人入住登记相关的英文词汇。 2. 掌握客人入住登记的服务程序及各个程序的英文表达。 3. 能用英文为有预订及无预订的散客提供入住登记服务。 4. 能用英文进行团队入住登记服务。 5. 通过训练，培养精益求精、吃苦耐劳的工匠精神		

头脑风暴

1. 前台工作人员为 Hanks 先生办理入住登记，需要哪些程序？
2. 如果 Hanks 先生没有预订，该如何为其办理入住登记？
3. 入住登记手续办理完成后，前台工作人员应告知客人哪些信息？

词汇储备

1. check in　登记
2. register　*v.* 登记　　registration　*n.* 登记
3. registration form/list　登记表
4. vacancy　*n.* 空房　（room available 空房）
5. room fee/charge　房价　（room rate=daily rate 房价）
6. sign　*v.* 签名　　signature　*n.* 签名
7. receipt　*n.* 收据
8. breakfast coupon　早餐券
9. credit card　信用卡
10. Wechat pay/pay by Wechat　微信付款
11. Alipay/ pay by Alipay　支付宝付款
12. scan the QR code　扫二维码
13. follow the official account　关注公众号

项目 1　The Front Office（前厅部）

服务流程

入住登记服务（有预订）流程如下：

1. Greetings.
   问候。
2. Asking the guest if he has a reservation.
   询问客人是否有预订。
3. Checking the reservation list/record.
   核对预订记录。
4. Asking the guest to show his identification and fill in the registration form.
   让客人出示证件并填写登记表。
5. Asking the guest the way of his payment.
   询问客人付款方式。
6. Giving the room key/card to the guest and telling some information.
   交给客人房卡，并告知客人一些入住信息。
7. Expressing the wishes.
   表达祝愿。

入住登记服务
（有预订）

入住登记服务（无预订）流程如下：

1. Greetings.
   问候。
2. Asking the guest if he has a reservation.
   询问客人是否有预订。
3. Asking the guest the accommodation request and checking the reservation list/record.
   询问客人其入住需求并核对预订记录。
4. Asking the guest to show his identification and fill in the registration form.
   让客人出示证件并填写登记表。
5. Asking the guest the way of his payment.
   询问客人付款方式。
6. Giving the room key/card to the guest and telling some information.
   交给客人房卡，并告知客人一些入住信息。
7. Expressing the wishes.
   表达祝愿。

入住登记服务
（无预订）

情境模拟

入住登记服务（有预订）

1. The first step: Greetings.
   第一步：问候。常用的句子有：

a. Good morning, welcome to our hotel. May I help you?
   早上好，欢迎来到我们的酒店，有什么能帮到您的？

b. Good afternoon, madam. How may I help you?
   下午好，女士。有什么能帮到您的？

c. Good evening, ladies and gentlemen. Welcome to Sofitel Hotel. Who is your tour leader?
   晚上好，女士们，先生们。欢迎来到索菲特酒店，请问谁是你们的领队？

d. Good morning. Sir. I am Tina. Welcome. What can I do for you?
   早上好，先生。我是 Tina。您需要什么帮助？

e. Good morning, sir/ madam. Receptions, what can I do for you?
   早上好，女士 / 先生。接待处，有什么能帮到您的？

情境 1： 下午 1 点左右，Miller 女士和 Hanks 先生一行人来到索菲特酒店前台，准备办理入住。

　　Good afternoon, ladies and gentlemen. Welcome to Sofitel Hotel. May I help you?

情境 2： 上午，一位男士来到前台，准备办理入住。

　　Good morning, sir. welcome to our hotel. How may I help you?

情境 3： 前台的 Jane 晚上接待了一位办理登记入住的女士。

　　Good evening, I am Jane. What can I do for you?

2. The second step: Asking the guest if he has a reservation.
   第二步：询问客人是否有预订。常用的句子有：

   a. Sir/Madam, do you have a reservation (with us)？
      先生 / 女士，您有预订吗？

   b. Sir/Madam, have you made a reservation (with us)？
      先生 / 女士，您有预订吗？

   c. Sir/Madam, have you reserved/booked a room?
      先生 / 女士，您有预订吗？

情境 1： 询问 Miller 女士和她的团队是否有预订。

　　Madam, do you have reservations?

情境 2： 询问一位来到前台准备办理入住的男士是否有预订。

　　Sir, have you made a reservation with us?

3. The third step: Checking the reservation list/record.
   第三步：核对预订记录。常用的句子有：

   a. Just a moment, please. I will check it.

b. Just a minute, please. I will check your reservation record.

c. Would you mind waiting a moment, let me check?

情境 1：让办理入住的 Miller 女士稍微等一会儿，查阅一些预订记录。

Just a moment, please. Ms Miller. I will check your reservation record.

情境 2：让办理入住的客人稍等一会儿。

Sir/Madam, just a moment, please. I will check it.

4. The fourth step: Asking the guest to show his identification and fill in the registration form.

第四步：让客人出示证件并填写登记表（可与客人确认一下预订信息）。常用的句子有：

a. May I see your passport, please?
我可以看一下您的护照吗？

b. May I have a look at/look at your passport, please?
我可以看一下您的护照吗？

c. Please show me your passport, madam.
请出示您的护照，女士。

d. Would you like to fill in/out the registration form?
请您填写一下登记表。（您能填写一些登记表吗？）

e. Do you mind filling out the registration form?
您介意填写一下登记表吗？（您能填写一些登记表吗？）

f. Please fill in the registration form and sign your name here.
请填写一下登记表，并在此处签名。

g. Don't forget to sign your name.
别忘记签上您的名字。

情境 1：让一位有预订的男性客人出示护照，并告知客人其预订了一间单人间，三晚。填写登记表并签名。

Sir, may I see your passport please? This is your registration form, you booked a single room for 3 nights. Please check it and sign your name here.

情境 2：让有预订的客人出示护照，并填写登记表。

Madam, please show me your passport and fill in/out the registration list and sign your name here.

5. The fifth step: Asking the guest the way of his payment.

第五步：询问客人付款方式。常用的句子有：

a. How would you like to pay?

您怎么付款？

b. How would you like to pay, in cash or by credit card?

您怎么付款，用现金还是信用卡？

c. How would you like to make your payment?

您怎么付款？

d. How would you like to pay for your deposit?

您怎么付您的押金？

情境 1： 接待员 Jane 接待了客人 Smith 先生，为其办理入住登记，询问其付款方式，Smith 先生要用现金支付押金。

R: Mr. Smith, how would you like to make your payment?

S: In cash.

情境 2： 接待员接待客人为其办理入住，询问其付款方式，并告知客人需要 1 300 元押金，客人要用信用卡支付。

R: Madam, How would you like to pay for your deposit? We require 1 300 Yuan.

G: By credit card.

R: May I have your credit card?

G: Here you are.

6. The sixth step: Giving the room key/card to the guest and telling some information.

第六步：交给客人房卡，并告知客人一些入住信息。常用的句子有：

a. Here is your key card to Room 1312. The bellman will show you the way.

这是您 1312 室的房卡，行李员会为您指引到您的房间。

b. This is your room key, please be careful with them. Your room is on the 8th floor. The bellboy will show you to your room with your luggage.

这是您的房间钥匙，请妥善保管。您的房间在 8 楼，行李员会为您指引，并把行李为您搬上去。

c. Here is your receipt and room card, please keep them. Your room is on the 16th floor. The bellman will deliver your luggage to your room.

这是您的收据和房卡，请您收好。您的房间在 16 楼。行李员会把您的行李搬上去。

d. Sir, here is your room card and breakfast coupon. Your room number is 808 and the breakfast time is from 6:30 a.m. to 10:30 a.m. at the Garden Restaurant on the 2nd floor. The bellboy will show you (up) to your room.

先生，这是您的房卡和早餐券，您的房间号码是 808。早餐时间是早 6：30 到早 10：30，在二楼的花园餐厅。行李员会指引您到房间。

情境1： 接待员告知客人房间号码为412，并递送房卡和早餐券。
Madam, you are in Room 412 and this is your room card and breakfast coupon.

情境2： 接待员把房卡和收据递送给客人，并告知客人行李员会为他指引房间。
Sir, here is your room card and the receipt, please keep them. The bellman will show you to your room.

情境3： 接待员为客人Smith先生办理好登记手续后，给Smith先生房卡和早餐券，并告知其早餐供应时间为早6点到早10点，供应地点为1楼的玫瑰餐厅。
Mr. Smith, your room number is 606, here is your room card and breakfast coupon. The breakfast is served from 6 a.m. to 10 a.m. in the Rose Restaurant on the 1st floor.

入住登记服务（无预订）

1. The first step: Greetings.
   第一步：问候。

2. The second step: Asking the guest if he has a reservation.
   第二步：询问客人是否有预订。

3. The third step: Asking the guest the accommodation request and checking the reservation list/record.

第三步：询问客人其入住需求并核对预订记录。常用的句子有：

   a. What kind/sort of room would you like?
      您想要住哪种房型？
   b. Let me check if there is any... (room type) available?
      我看看是否有空的……？（房型）
   c. Let me check the reservation list/record.
      我看一下我们的预订记录。
   d. One moment, please. Let me see...（checking room available）
      请您稍等，让我看看我们的……（查看一下是否有空房）
   e. How many nights would you like to stay?
      您打算住几晚？
   f. For how many nights?
      您住几晚？
   g. Do you have any special requests?
      您有什么特殊需求吗？

情境1： 一位无预订散客来到索菲特酒店的前台，准备入住一间单人间，接待员为其办理。
Sir, just a moment, please. I will check if there is any single room available? Thanks for your waiting. We have a single room.

情境 2：两位无预订客人准备入住索菲特酒店。

  R: What kind of room would you like?

  G: A family suite.

  R: One moment, please. Let me see... we have a family suite. And the room rate is 580 Yuan per night. Is that OK?

4. The fourth step: Asking the guest to show his identification and fill in the registration form.

   第四步：让客人出示证件并填写登记表（可与客人确认一下预订信息）。

5. The fifth step: Asking the guest the way of his payment.

   第五步：询问客人付款方式。

6. The sixth step: Giving the room key/card to the guest and telling some information.

   第六步：交给客人房卡，并告知客人一些入住信息。

能力进阶

团队客人来到前台准备办理入住登记，服务程序及常用的句子有：

1. Greetings.

   问候。

2. Asking the guest's name or the way of the reservation.

   询问客人是以谁的名字预订的或询问客人是以何种方式预订的。

   a. In whose name was the reservation made?

     您是以谁的名字预订的？

   b. In which way was the reservation made?

     您是以何种方式预订的？

   c. Was the reservation made in John Smith?

     您是以 John Smith 先生的名字预订的吗？

   d. What was the date of the reservation?

     您是哪天预订的？

延长预订服务

3. Checking the information (in the computer).

   核对预订记录。

4. Asking the guest's request.

   询问客人（新的）需求。

   a. How would you like to change/revise?

     您想如何更改？

   b. How would like to change your previous reservation?

     您想如何更改您之前的预订？

项目 1　The Front Office（前厅部）

  c. How to change please, sir?

   先生，您想如何更改？

  d. Would you like to extend your reservation for two more nights?

   你想再延长预订两晚吗？

5. Confirming reservation.

  确认信息。

  a. I will change/cancel/extend your reservation for you.

   我将为您更改 / 取消 / 延长您的预订。

  b. Mr. Smith, I will cancel your reservation for July, 5th for three nights. My name is Tina. Glad to be of your service.

   Smith 先生，我为您取消 7 月 5 号起三晚的预订。我是 Tina。很高兴为您服务。

6. Expressing the wishes.

  表达祝愿。

  a. We look forward to another chance to serve you.

   （针对取消预订）我们期待着再有机会为您服务。

  b. We look forward to having another opportunity to serve you.

   （针对取消预订）我们期待着再有机会为您服务。

当酒店客房预订已满时，常用的句子有：

  a. I'm sorry, but we are fully booked on that date.

   很抱歉，我们那天的客房预订已满。

  b. All of our rooms are fully booked/occupied. We're very sorry, sir. We hope you could understand us.

   很抱歉先生，我们所有的客房预订已满，希望得到您的理解。

  c. Sir, how about a single room, the suite are fully booked now.

   先生，单人间怎么样？套房现在预订已满。

  d. Sir, if you like, I would like to suggest another hotel which is near ours.

   先生，如果您不介意，我为您推荐离我们距离很近的其他酒店行吗？

语言使用

讲礼貌 being polite——交流中使用的礼貌语言

  礼貌用语的使用在服务业中是至关重要的。作为从事服务业的工作人员，我们要知道如何使用英语礼貌用语。下面这些英文表达可以使你的语言听起来更加礼貌。

1. 向客人提出问题时：Could /Would you please tell me...

  询问客人何时离店：

  a. When do you want to leave? 错（不礼貌，有催促客人马上离开的意思）

  b. Could you please tell me when you leave? 对

  c. Would you please tell me your departure date? 对

17

2. 当拒绝客人提出的要求，或不能满足客人的要求时：I am afraid that... 或 I am afraid to tell you...

    告知客人双人房没有了：

    a. There isn't any double rooms available. 错（比较粗鲁，有冒犯客人之意）

    b. I am afraid that there isn't any double rooms available. 对

3. 当客人挡路时：Excuse me 开头

    a. Move out of the way. 错（语气粗鲁，容易遭到别人的拒绝）

    b. Excuse me, sir...

4. 阻止客人做一些事情时，可对使用 Would you mind not... 开头告知客人不能在会议室里大声说话。

    a. Stop talking in the meeting room. 错（粗鲁，会激怒客人）

    b. Would you mind not talking loudly in the meeting room? 对

5. 电话用语中，可在开头加上 Would/ Could you...?

    打电话时，告知客人等待

    a. Wait. 错（不礼貌）

    b. Could/Would you hold on, please? 对

能力训练

情境 1：

Miller 女士一周前通过电话预订的方式在沈阳丽都索菲特酒店预订了三间商务套房。今天上午，她来到沈阳丽都索菲特酒店。刚进大堂，接待员接待了他们并为他们办理了入住登记手续……

Miss Miller made a reservation of a business suite a week ago, now she is at the reception desk...

要求：①两人一组，完成对话；
②注意服务礼仪及英文礼貌用语的使用。

情境 2：

Jennifer 女士到沈阳旅游，想要入住沈阳丽都索菲特酒店，但是她事先没有预订，Jennifer 来到的酒店的大堂，准备办理入住登记手续，接待员接待了她。

Ms Jennifer...

要求：①两人一组，完成对话；
②注意服务礼仪及英文礼貌用语的使用。

项目 1　The Front Office（前厅部）

学习任务 3　Exchanging Foreign Currency（外币兑换服务）

工作任务	Exchanging Foreign Currency（外币兑换服务）	教学模式	线上线下混合教学模式 情境模拟教学模式
建议学时	4 学时	教学地点	智慧教室或多媒体教室
任务描述	Hanks 先生来到服务台，说他看到酒店商务中心里的宝石饰品不错，想购买一些作纪念品，需要兑换 4 000 元人民币		
学习目标	1. 掌握外币兑换的服务流程。 2. 掌握服务程序中常用的英文语句。 3. 能够准确无误地用英文表达外币。 4. 能够熟练地用英文做外币兑换服务。 5. 能够指导客人到酒店外的银行兑换外币。 6. 通过训练，培养学生团结协作、有效沟通的能力。 7. 通过训练，培养学生认真、严谨、敬业的工作作风		

头脑风暴

1. 你了解哪些国家的货币和货币符号？它们用英文怎么说？
2. 你知道酒店外币兑换的流程是怎样的？
3. 如果客人要求的货币在酒店无法兑换，你该如何处理？

词汇储备

1. Cash Desk=Cashier Counter　收银台
2. cash　*n.* 现金
3. cashier　*n.* 收银员
4. currency　*n.* 货币
5. foreign currency/ foreign currencies　外币
6. exchange　*v.&n.* 交换，兑换
7. exchange rate　兑换率
8. exchange memo　外币兑换水单
9. traveler's check　旅行支票
10. according to　根据

服务流程

服务流程如下：

1. Greetings.
   问候。

外币兑换服务

19

2. Introducing today's exchange rate to the guest.
   向客人介绍今天的汇率。

3. Asking the guest how much he wants to change and receiving the money from the guest.
   询问客人想要兑换的金额并收钱。

4. Checking the guest's passport.
   核对客人的护照。

5. Asking the guest to fill in the exchange memo and asking him/her to sign the name.
   让客人填写兑换单并签名。

6. Telling the guest about the amout of money and asking him to count.
   告诉客人兑换后的金额并让客人点钞核对。

7. Giving the exchange memo to the guest and asking him to keep it well.
   把兑换单给客人并告诉客人保存好。

8. Expressing the wishes.
   表达祝愿。

情境模拟

1. The first step: Greetings.
   第一步：问候。常用的句子有：

   a. Good morning, sir/ madam. What can I do for you?

   b. Good morning, sir/ madam. May I help you?

   c. Good morning, sir/ madam. Is there anything I can do for you?

   d. Good morning, sir/ madam. How may I help you?

   情境 1： 住店客人 Hanks 先生来到服务台，想兑换一些人民币。
   Good morning, Mr. Hanks. What can I do for you?

   情境 2： Smith 先生下午来到酒店前台，想要兑换一些人民币。
   Good afternoon, sir. May I help you?

2. The second step: Introducing today's exchange rate to the guest.
   第二步：向客人介绍今天的汇率。常用的句子有：

   a. Today's exchange rate is 7.05 Yuan RMB for one US dollar.
      今天的汇率是每一美元可换成 7.05 元人民币。

   b. According to today's exchange rate, one US dollar in cash comes to 7.05 RMB.
      根据今天的汇率，每 1 美元的现金可以兑换成 7.05 人民币。

   c. The exchange rate of US dollar to RMB is 1:6.70.
      汇率是每一美元可换成 6.70 元的人民币。

项目 1　The Front Office（前厅部）

情境 1： 住店客人 Hanks 先生在房间打电话到前台，他想要询问欧元兑换人民币汇率情况。

　　Mr. Hanks, at today's exchange rate, 1 euro comes to 10.05 RMB.

情境 2： 向 Smith 先生解答今天美元汇率情况。

　　Mr. Smith, today's exchange rate is 7.05 Yuan for one US dollar.

3. The third step: Asking the guest how much he wants to change and receiving the money from the guest.

　　第三步：询问客人想要兑换的金额并收钱。常用的句子有：

　　a. How much would you like to change, sir /madam?
　　　您想要换多少？

　　b. How much, sir /madam?
　　　您想要换多少？

情境 1： 询问住店客人 Hanks 先生想要兑换的金额。

　　How much would you like to change, Mr. Hanks?

情境 2： 前台 Helen 询问 Smith 先生想要兑换的金额。

　　How much would you like to change, Mr. Smith?

4. The fourth step: Checking the guest's passport.

　　第四步：核对客人的护照。常用的句子有：

　　a. May I have a look at your passport, sir?

　　b. May I look at your passport, madam?

　　c. May I see your passport, sir?
　　　先生 / 女士，能让我看看你的护照吗？

情境 1： 前台 Helen 请住店客人 Hanks 先生出示护照。

　　So, Mr. Hanks, may I have a look at your passport, please?

情境 2： 前台 Helen 请 Miller 女士出示护照。

　　May I look at your passport, madam?

5. The fifth step: Asking the guest to fill in the exchange memo and asking him/her to sign the name.

　　第五步：让客人填写兑换单并签名。常用的句子有：

　　a. Please fill in the exchange memo—your passport number, the total sum, room number or permanent address and sign your name.

　　请您填写外汇水单——填写上您的护照号、兑换金额、房间号或永久性地址，并签上您的名字。

    b. Would you please fill in the exchange memo?

    c. Would you mind filling in the exchange memo?

       请您填写外汇水单，好吗？

    d. Please sign your name here.

    e. Don't forget to sign your name here.

       请签上您的名字。

情境 1： 住店客人 Hanks 先生填写水单并签名。

       Mr. Hanks, Please fill in the exchange memo—your passport number, the total sum, room number or permanent address and sign your name.

情境 2： Miller 女士填写水单并签名。

       Would you please fill in the exchange memo and sign your name here madam?

6. The sixth step: Telling the guest about the amount of money and asking him to count.

   第六步：告诉客人兑换后的金额并让客人点钞核对。常用的句子有：

    a. What denominations would you like?

       您想要哪种面值的货币？

    b. In which denominations?

       哪种面值？

    c. How would you like your money?

       您要什么面值的货币？

    d. Here/The sum is...Yuan. Please count it.

       这是……元，请点一下。

情境 1： 按照当天汇率，前台 Helen 递给 Hanks 先生 2 000 元人民币。

       Mr. Hanks, here is RMB 2 000. Please count it.

情境 2： Miller 女士兑换到 600 元人民币。

       Here is RMB 600. Please count it, madam.

7. The seventh step: Giving the exchange memo to the guest and asking him to keep it well.

   第七步：把兑换单给客人并告诉客人保存好。常用的句子有：

   Here's your memo. Please keep it well.

8. The eighth step: Expressing the wishes.

   第八步：表达祝愿。常用的句子有：

   Glad to serve you.

   很高兴为您服务。

情境 1：前台 Helen 递给 Hanks 先生水单并嘱咐他保存好。

　　　　Mr. Hanks, Here's your memo. Please keep it well. Glad to serve you.

情境 2：Miller 女士收到兑换单。

　　　　Here's your memo. Please keep it well. Glad to serve you, madam.

能力进阶

酒店不能为客人提供外币兑换服务，建议客人到中国银行兑换。常用的句子有：

a. I'm afraid that you'll have to change it at the Bank of China.
　　恐怕您得到中国银行去兑换。

b. If we change large amounts, our cash supply may run out and we won't be able to serve our other guests.
　　如果我们兑换大额钱币，我们的现金可能会不够从而不能为其他客人服务。

c. I do apologize for it.
　　非常抱歉。

语言使用

Look forward to 主要用法

1. look forward to +n. 期待某物
   e.g.: We look forward to your news.
   我们期待你的消息。

2. look forward to +doing sth. 期待做某事
   e.g.: We look forward to serving you.
   我们期待着为您服务。

能力训练

情境 1：

Hanks 先生来到服务台，想兑换 20 万元人民币。服务员告诉客人酒店如果进行大额兑换，就可能造成资金短缺，那么酒店就不能为其他客人提供外币兑换服务了。所以建议客人到中国人民银行兑换。

要求：以小组为单位总结出服务员的英文应对语句。

情境 2：

Hanks 先生来到服务台，想兑换人民币。服务员按照流程给他办理，期间，特别告诉客人在填写外币兑换水单时的填写内容和注意事项。

要求：以小组为单位总结出服务员的英文应对语句。

学习任务 4　Check Out（结账退宿服务）

工作任务	Check Out（结账退宿服务）	教学模式	线上线下混合教学模式 情境模拟教学模式
建议学时	4 学时	教学地点	智慧教室或多媒体教室
任务描述	Hanks 先生等一行七人入住沈阳丽都索菲特酒店后，对酒店提供的接待、餐饮及商务服务都非常满意。今天，Hanks 先生来到前台办理结账离店服务		
学习目标	1. 掌握结账退宿服务的流程。 2. 掌握服务流程中常用的英文语句。 3. 能够熟练地用英文给客人做结账退宿服务。 4. 能够准确无误地用英文与客人沟通付款方式。 5. 能够处理结账退宿服务中遇到的突发事件。 6. 通过训练，培养学生团结协作、有效沟通的能力。 7. 通过训练，培养学生认真、严谨、敬业的工作作风		

头脑风暴

1. 你了解账单上常用的一些英文缩写吗？
2. 给客人办理结账退宿的服务流程是什么，各个程序应如何与客人进行英语沟通？
3. 如果账单有误，怎么与客人沟通处理？

词汇储备

1. check out　结账离店 结账退宿
2. credit card　信用卡
3. service charge　服务费
4. deposit　*n.* 押金
5. invoice　*n.* 发票
6. change　*n.* 零钱
7. cash　*n.* 现金
8. cashier　*n.* 收银员
9. bill　*n.* 账单
10. draw up　结算
11. 15 percent　15%
12. calculate　*v.* 计算

账单上常用英文缩写词汇

Room= room charge /room rate　房费

T= Telephone Call Charge　电话费

L.DIST= Long distance call　长途电话费

RESTR= Restaurant　餐饮费

L= laundry　洗衣费

MISC=miscellaneous　杂费

P.I.A.= paid in advance　已预付

C.I.A.=cash in advance　预付现金

B.N.P.=bill not paid　未结账

服务流程

结账退宿服务

1. The first step: Greetings.

    第一步：问候。常用的句子有：

    a. Good morning, sir/ madam. What can I do for you?

    b. Good morning, sir/ madam. May I help you?

    c. Good morning, sir/ madam. Is there anything I can do for you?

    d. Good morning, sir/ madam. How may I help you?

        上午好，先生/女士，有什么可以为您效劳的？

2. The second step: asking the guest the name and the room number and give you the room (key) card.

    第二步：询问客人姓名和房间号并索要房卡。常用的句子有：

    a. May I have your name, your room number and room card please?

    b. May I know your name, your room number and room card please?

        您的姓名和房间号码是什么？请拿出您的房卡。

情境 1：上午 9 点，住在 2608 房间的 Hanks 先生来到前台结账退宿。

　　Good morning, Mr. Hanks. May I have your name and room number please?

情境 2：Miller 女士来到前台，为住在 2316 房的 Smith 先生办理退宿手续。

　　Good morning, madam. Would you please tell me your name and room number?

3. The third step: drawing up the bill.

    第三步：结算账单。常用的句子有：

    a. Just a moment, please. Thanks for waiting so long, sir /madam?

        请稍等，谢谢您，让您久等了。

    b. Wait a moment, please. sir /madam? I'll draw up the bill for you.

        您请等一会儿，我给您结账。

4. The fourth step: Telling the total and give the bill to the guest for checking
   第四步：告诉客人总额并让客人核对账单。常用的句子有：
   a. Here's your bill. The total is 2 465 Yuan RMB. Please check it.
   b. Your bill please. it comes to 2 465 Yuan RMB. Would you like to check it?
   c. Your bill totals 2 465 Yuan RMB. Please check it.
   d. Here's your bill, 2 465 Yuan RMB in all. Please check it.
      这是您的账单，共计 2 465 元，请核对。

情境 1： 告知住店客人 Hanks 先生共消费 2 680 元。
   Mr.Smith, Your bill totals 2 680 Yuan RMB. Please check it.
情境 2： 前台工作人员告诉 Miller 女士，2316 房共消费 2 465 元。
   Madam, Your bill please. it comes to 2 465 Yuan RMB. Would you like to check it?

5. The fifth step: Explaining the items if necessary.
   第五步：如果需要，给客人解释明细。常用的句子有：
   a. There is 10% service charge for the express service.
      快洗服务有 10% 的服务费。
   b. Would you please fill in the exchange memo.
      您能填写一下兑换水单吗？

情境 1： Hanks 先生在账单上发现有 50 元的消费，他询问工作人员明细。
   H: What's this 50 Yuan for?
   C: It's the Service charge for room service.
   H: I see. Thank you.
情境 2： 为一位女客人解释两处账单明细。
   Madam, this "L" is for Laundry and this "Room" is for room service.

6. The sixth step: Asking the guest how to pay and handle making the payment.
   第六步：询问客人支付方式并收款。常用的句子有：
   a. How will you be paying?
   b. How would you like to pay?
      您怎样付款？

情境 1： 前台工作人员询问住店客人 Hanks 先生的付款方式。
   Mr. Hanks, How would you like to pay?
情境 2： 前台工作人员询问 Miller 女士的付款方式。
   How will you be paying? Madam.

项目 1　The Front Office（前厅部）

7. The seventh step: Expressing the wishes.

   第七步：告别并表达祝愿。常用的句子有：

   a. We hope you'll be staying with us again. Have a nice trip.
      希望您下次光临我们酒店。祝您旅途愉快。
   b. We hope you've enjoyed your stay in the hotel. Hope you enjoy your trip.
      希望您对我们的服务满意。祝您旅途愉快。
   c. We hope we have another opportunity to serve you.
      希望能再有机会为您服务。

能力进阶

酒店前台工作人员算错客人账单，给客人改账并道歉，常用的句子有：

a. You've been overcharged. Please wait a moment, I'll check it.
   多收您钱了，请稍候，我会核对一下。
b. Don't worry. Wait a moment please.
   不用担心，请稍候。
c. We are terribly sorry for overcharging you. I must apologize for the inconvenience.
   我们十分抱歉多收您钱款。我们为给您带来的不便道歉。
d. We'll return the money you have overpaid.
   多收的钱款我们会退还给您的。

语言使用

enjoy 的主要用法

1. enjoy +sth. 很喜欢某事（某物）

   e.g.: Hope you enjoy your stay here.
   希望你入住愉快。

2. enjoy +doing sth. 很喜欢做某事

   e.g.: He enjoys playing basketball.
   他很喜欢打篮球。

3. enjoy +oneself 玩得开心

   e.g.: He enjoyed himself at the party.
   他在晚会上玩得很开心。

能力训练

情境 1：

中午 12 点，Hanks 先生来到前台办理结账退宿。他在办理入住时已经预付押金 1 000 元人民币，账单总额为 2 829 元，客人要求现金结账。

要求：以小组为单位总结出服务员的英文应对语句。

情境 2：

中午 12 点，Hanks 先生来到前台办理结账退宿。客人共消费 1 465 元，酒店接受美国运通卡、万事达卡、维萨卡、联邦卡，客人想用运通卡付款，服务员告诉客人，如果要使用信用卡买单，他要付 5% 的贸易商委托费。

要求：以小组为单位总结出服务员的英文应对语句。

能力拓展

前厅服务英语 200 句

1. Good morning. Reservation. May I help you? / What can I do for you?
   你好，预订部，有什么可以帮到您的吗？

2. Good afternoon, welcome to Hilton Hotel! May I help you?
   下午好，欢迎光临希尔顿酒店，我可以帮您吗？

3. Hold on, please. /Could you please hold on?
   请稍等。/ 您能等一下吗？

4. Could you wait a minute, please?
   请稍等，好吗？

5. I'd like to book a single room for Wednesday next week.
   我想要订一间下周三入住的单人间。

6. I'd like to book a double room for my friend.
   我想为朋友预订一间双人间。

7. I'd like to reserve rooms for my group.
   我想团体预订。

8. We offer 10% discount for group reservation, sir.
   先生，团队预订可以打九折。

9. I want a double room with a bath.
   我要一间有浴室的双人房。

10. We will take two smoking connecting room.
    我们需要 2 个可以抽烟的相邻的房间。

11. Do you have a room with a nice view?
    有风景好一点的房间吗？

12. Could you repeat that, please?

请您重复一遍好吗？

13. Beg your pardon?
    对不起请再说一遍好吗？

14. How long will you plan to stay?
    请问您住几天？

15. How long will you be staying?
    请问您住几天？

16. How long will you stay with us?
    请问您住几天？

17. May I know your departure date?
    请问您的离店日期是哪天？

18. May I know the arrival date, please?
    请问哪天入住？

19. How many people are there in your party?
    你们一共几个人？

20. When would you like to check in?
    请问您什么时候入住？

21. We'll extend the reservation for you.
    我们可以为您延长预订。

22. Would you like a single room or a double room/TWB/suite?
    请问您想订单人间还是双人间/标准间/套房？

23. What kind of room would you like/prefer?
    请问您喜欢什么样的房间？

24. I'm afraid we have no triple rooms, but we can put an extra bed into one of our double room. would that suit you?
    很抱歉，我们没有三人间，但是我们能在双人间里放一张床，可以吗？

25. Would you please tell me your full name, please?
    请问您的全名是……？

26. May I know/have your name, please?
    请问你的名字是……？

27. Excuse me, sir, could you spell your name?
    请问您的名字如何拼写？

28. And your address, please?
    请问您的地址是……？

29. May I know your company name and how would you like to settle your payment?
    请问您的公司全称及付款方式是……？

30. How would you like to guarantee your reservation?

请问您的担保方式是……？

31. May I know/have your telephone number, Mr. White?
怀特先生，请问您的电话号码是……？

32. Please wait a moment. I have to check if there is a room available.
请稍等，我查一下有没有空房。

33. We do have a vacancy for those dates.
那段时间我们可以接受预订。

34. I'm afraid we won't be able to guarantee you a room after the 16th. We usually have high occupancies in the peak seasons.
恐怕16号后我们不能保证有房间提供给您，那段时间是我们的入住高峰期。

35. We have a single available for those dates.
我们还有一些单人间可以在那个时间段接受预订。

36. We charge RMB 600 for a deluxe twin per night.
豪华双人间，每间每天600元。

37. we can do a single/double/TWB room for RMB 350 per night.
单人间/双人间/标准间，每间每天350元。

38. How much does a double room cost?
一间双人房要多少钱？

39. How much a day do you charge?
每天房费是多少？

40. What's the rate?
房价是多少？

41. Can I get a discount?
有优惠吗？/有折扣吗？

42. What's the price difference?
价格有什么不同？

43. Do you have an inexpensive / cheaper room?
有便宜一点的房间吗？

44. Do you have a better room?
有好一点的房间吗？

45. Please give me a less expensive room.
请给我一个便宜一点的房间。

46. With a front view or a rear view?
阴面还是阳面？（指客房）

47. It is one hundred Yuan a day including heating fee, but excluding service charge.
100元一天，包括供暖费，但不包括服务费。

48. A double room with a front view is 140 dollars per night, one with a rear view is 115

dollars per night.

阳面双人房每晚 140 美元，阴面每晚 115 美元。

49. It's quite reasonable.

    收费十分合理。

50. May I know your company name and how would you like to settle your payment?

    请问您的公司全称及付款方式是……？

51. Service isn't included in the room rate.

    服务费不包含在房费里。

52. We offer 10% discount for group reservation, sir.

    先生，团队预订可以打九折。

53. I'm sorry, there is no discount.

    对不起，我们不提供折扣。

54. There's a reduction for children.

    儿童可以减价。

55. We have already cut the price very fine.

    我们已经将价格降至最低了。

56. Would you mind waiting for a few moment?

    请您等一会好吗？

57. Could you hold on a minute?

    请稍等（电话用语）。

58. Cloud you please hold on?

    请稍等（电话用语）。

59. Would you mind waiting for a few moment?

    请您等一会好吗？

60. Would you please pay 1 000 Yuan as deposit? We will return the balance to you when you check out.

    请您付 1 000 元押金，我们将在您退房时将余额退还给您。

61. I'm sorry, but we're fully booked for single rooms. Would you like to have a double one?

    很抱歉，我们的单人间已经订满了，双人间怎么样？

62. I'm afraid our hotel is fully booked on that date.

    对不起，我们酒店那一天的客房全部订满了。

63. I'm sorry, we don't have any room available for that week.

    很抱歉，我们那周的预订已经全满。

64. I'm sorry, but we are fully booked up.

    很抱歉，我们没有空房。

65. I'm sorry, but we have no vacancies at that moment.

对不起，我们现在没有空房。

66. I'm sorry, but all rooms are taken.
    很抱歉，所有的客房都已经订满了。

67. Your room is confirmed for that day. We look forward to serving you.
    您要的那一日房间已经确认了，我们期待为您服务。

68. Do you mind sharing a room with other people?
    请问您介意与他人共享一个房间吗？

69. I suggest you make a reservation now, because there's a special discount.
    我建议您预订一个房间，现在有优惠。

70. Mr. smith, let me repeat your reservation to ensure it is correct. you will arrive before...
    史密斯先生，我跟你确认一下你的预订内容：你的抵达日期是……

71. I hope you will enjoy your stay here.
    希望您将有一个愉快的入住。

72. Mind (watch) your step.
    请走好。

73. Be careful as you step down.
    下车时请小心。

74. Is this all your luggage?
    这些就是您全部的行李吗？

75. May I take your bag for you?
    我可以为您拿手提包吗？

76. May I help you with your suitcase?
    我可以帮您拿箱子吗？

77. So you've got altogether three pieces of luggage.
    您一共有三件行李。

78. Your entire luggage is here, seven pieces in all.
    您的行李都在这里，共七件。

79. Are these your luggage? May I take them for you?
    这些是您的行李吗？我来帮您拿好吗？

80. Excuse me, is this bag yours?
    请问，这个行李是您的吗？

81. I've come for your luggage.
    我来帮您提行李。

82. How many pieces (of luggage) do you have?
    请问您一共有几件行李？

83. Sorry, we can't accept tips in our hotel. Thank you all the same.
    对不起，我们酒店不允许接受小费，但还是谢谢您。

84. This way please.
    请走这边。

85. Would you care to step this way?
    请这边走，好吗？

86. After you, please.
    您先请。

87. The Reception Desk is straight ahead.
    接待处就在前面。

88. The Reception Desk is over there.
    接待处就在那边。

89. Have you a got a reservation?
    您预订过了吗？

90. Have you made a reservation?
    您预订过了吗？

91. Just a moment, sir. While I look through our list.
    请等一下，我看看我们的记录。

92. Have you reserved a room?
    您预订过了吗？

93. Let me have a check again.
    让我再看一下。

94. You must be Professor Brown.
    您一定是布朗教授吧。

95. You've paid 2 000 Yuan RMB as a deposit. Is that correct?
    您付了定金 2 000 元，对吗？

96. May I know your nationality?
    请问您的国籍是哪里？

97. May I have/know your check out time?
    请问您什么时候结账离开？

98. Could you please fill out this form?
    请您填写一下这张表格，好吗？

99. May i see your passport, please?
    我可以看看您的护照吗？

100. 请 Would you please complete this registration form?
     请您填写这张登记表好吗？

101. Ok, I'll take good care of it.
     好的，我会好好填写的。

102. Could you please write them down?

请您写下来好吗?

103. May I have your passport or ID Card please?
请出示您的护照或身份证。

104. Please write your permanent address/forwarding address.
请填上您的永久地址/当前地址。

105. Please sign your name here.
请在此签名。

106. Sorry to have kept you waiting.
抱歉让您久等了。

107. I'll put in the room number for you later.
我一会为您填上房间号。

108. Please don't leave anything behind.
请别遗忘您的东西。

109. Take it easy!
放心好了!

110. If there's anything you need, please call the reception.
如果您需要什么,就打电话给接待处。

111. Would you please pay 1 000 Yuan as deposit? We will return the balance to you when you check out.
请您付 1 000 元押金,我们将在您退房时将余额退还您。

112. Here is your room key.
这是您的房间钥匙。

113. Here's your key to room 1220.
这是您 1220 房间的钥匙。

114. Your room number is 246 on the second floor.
您的房间在二楼的 246 房。

115. Here is your key card.
这是您的房卡。

116. Here is your room key.
这是您的房间钥匙。

117. please take good care of your key. We will charge 50 Yuan for the card if you lost it.
请保管好钥匙,如果丢失,我们将罚款 50 元。

118. please check out before 12 in the afternoon.
请您在 12 点前结账。

119. Your room number is 246 on the second floor.
您的房间在二楼的 246 房。

120. The bellman will show you the way to your room.

行李员将领您去您的房间。

121. The bellman will show you the way to the banquet hall.
行李员将领您去宴会厅。

122. The bellman here will take your luggage and show you the way.
这里的行李员会为您提行李，并为您带路。

123. I'll get the bellman to take your luggage up.
我会叫行李生帮您把行李送到房间。

124. Wish you a most pleasant stay in our hotel.
愿您在我们宾馆过得愉快。

125. I hope you will enjoy your stay with us.
希望您在我们宾馆过得愉快。（客人刚入店时）

126. I hope you are enjoying your stay with us。
希望您在我们宾馆过得愉快。（客人在酒店逗留期间）

127. I hope you have enjoyed your stay with us.
希望您在我们宾馆过得愉快。（客人将要离开酒店）

128. Excuse me, sir. I'm the bellboy. Do you need any help?
对不起，先生．我是行李员，请问需要帮忙吗？

129. This is your room. Here are your keys.
这就是您的房间．这是钥匙。

130. May I have your key, please? Let me open the door for you please.
请把钥匙给我，好吗？我为您开门。

131. It is a lovely room.
这真是一个漂亮的房间啊。

132. I'm glad you like it.
很高兴，您喜欢这个房间。

133. Where could I leave your luggage?
请问我应该把行李放在哪里？

134. May I show you the room facilities?
我给您介绍一下房间的设施，好吗？

135. Here is a brochure explaining hotel services.
这里有个小册子介绍饭店的各项服务。

136. Is there anything I can do for you before I leave the room?
在我离开之前，还有什么我能帮助您的吗？

137. If you need anything, please don't hesitate to tell us.
如果有什么需要，请告诉我们。

138. This is the remote control. There are ten channels including three English programs.
这里是遥控器，有10个频道，其中包括3个英文节目。

139. If you want to have your room cleaned extra quickly, please hang the Cleaning Sign on the door.

　　　如果您希望您的房间早些整理好，请将"请打扫"的牌子挂在门上。

140. There is a recreation center on the ground floor.

　　　一楼有一个娱乐中心。

141. Shall I turn the cooling up?

　　　我把冷气开大些，好吗？

142. Shall I turn the heating down?

　　　我把暖气开小些，好吗？

143. We have a sauna bath with a massage service there, too.

　　　我们还有桑拿浴室并提供按摩服务。

144. Are you checking out today?

　　　您今天要退房结账吗？

145. Are you leaving today?

　　　您今天退房吗？

146. Would you like to check out now?

　　　您现在退房结账吗？

147. Please wait your turn.

　　　请排队等候。

148. Do I have to pay rent for today if I will leave in the afternoon?

　　　如果我下午走，还要付当天的房租吗？

149. It depends on when you leave. If you leave after 12 o'clock, you have to pay half of the day's rent. If you leave after 6 p.m., you have to pay the full rent.

　　　那要看您几点离开了，如果中午十二点以后走，您得付一半；如果晚六点以后走，您就得付全天的。

150. According to hotel regulations, the time limit for setting accounts is at noon. If a guest leaves his room between 12 noon and 6 p.m., he must pay half a day's rent extra.

　　　饭店规定以中午十二点作为计算房金的时间界限，超过十二点要加收半天房租。

151. You arrived on May 1 and departure date is May 3，is it correct?

　　　您是5月1日入住，离店日期是5月3日，对吗？

152. Here is your bill to check and see if there are any mistakes.

　　　这是您的账单，请核对一下，看看是否有误。

153. Please pay at the cashier's desk over there.

　　　请到那边账台付款。

154. Please wait a moment while I calculate your bill.

　　　请稍等片刻，我立刻就把您的账单结算出来。

155. The total for the eight days is five hundred and fifty Yuan.

八天一共是 550 元。

156. Sorry, these two bills have not been included./ Sorry, I've forgotten to collect these two bills.

对不起，刚才漏收您两张账单。

157. How would you like to make payment, by credit card or in cash?

请问您想用现金付款还是用信用卡付款？

158. How do you like to pay your bill? In cash, with check or by credit card.

请问您要以何种方式付账，现金、支票还是信用卡？

159. How do you wish to pay your bill? In cash, with check or by credit card.

请问您希望以何种方式付账，现金、支票还是信用卡？

160. What's your idea to pay your bill? In cash, with check or by credit card.

请问您要以何种方式付账，现金、支票还是信用卡？

161. What's your way to pay your bill? In cash, with check or by credit card.

请问您要以何种方式付账，现金、支票还是信用卡？

162. We accept the following credit cards, madam.

女士，我们接受以下几种信用卡。

163. What kind of credit card do you have?

您的是哪种信用卡？

164. Here is your receipt.

这是您的收据。

165. Here is the money you overpaid.

这是退给您的钱。

166. Here is the change and your invoice. Keep this exchange memo.

这是您的发票和找零。请保管好您的兑换水单。

167. Would you please exchange us dollars for RMB, please?

麻烦你替我将美元兑成人民币好吗？

168. We do offer exchange service.

我们可以提供外币兑换服务。

169. how much would you like to exchange?

请问您要兑换多少？

170. The rates of exchange are on the board, sir.

先生，请参考告示牌的外币兑换价。

171. We can only change the foreign currencies listed on the foreign currency board. If you have other currencies to change, please go to the bank.

我们只能兑换外汇牌上的这些外币，其他外币您可以去银行兑换。

172. I'm sorry but we can't not exchange Hong Kong dollars into Japanese yen.

对不起，我们不能将港币换成日元。

173. Is there any place in the hotel where we can amuse ourselves?
    酒店里有供我们娱乐/打发时间的地方吗？

174. Yes of course. What can I do for you?
    当然可以。我能为您做些什么？

175. There are four flights every day. The plane takes off at about …respectively.
    共有4趟航班，飞机起飞的时间分别是……

176. The kids were disappointed that the pool wasn't open this morning, though.
    今天游泳池没有开，孩子们非常失望。

177. Would you please tell me the daily service hours of the dining room?
    请问能告诉我餐厅日常营业的时间吗？

178. Certainly./Of course./Sure.
    当然可以。

179. There is a recreation center on the ground (first) floor.
    在一楼有一个娱乐中心。

180. Excuse me, where can I buy some souvenirs?
    打扰一下，哪里可以买到纪念品？

181. There is a counter selling all kinds of souvenir over there.
    那边有一个柜台出售各种各样的纪念品。

182. Excuse me, sir. Do you mean you lost your room key?
    对不起，先生，您是不是说您把房间钥匙丢了？

183. Sorry, he isn't in at the moment.
    很抱歉，他现在不在。

184. Would you like to leave a message?
    您要留口信吗？

185. May I take a message for you?
    我可以为您捎个口信吗？

186. No problem, sir.
    没问题，先生。

187. We'll manage it, but we don't have any spare room today.
    我们会尽力办到，但是今天我们没有空余房间。

188. Could you wait till tomorrow?
    等到明天好吗？

189. Shall we solve the problem first? Later, we'll make clear who should take the responsibility.
    我们先不要讨论是谁的责任，先解决问题，好吗？

190. We will improve our service and business by training our staff more.
    我们会对员工加强培训，提高服务水平和业务水平。

191. We understand that you broke it unintentionally. But it did bring damages to the hotel, so compensation should be made.

我们都知道您不是故意损坏的，但这确实给酒店带来了损失，您应该给酒店相应的补偿。

192. We are sorry, but in this case we'd better not call the police for you, because we didn't witness the whole process and we can't make clear all the details to the police. Please dial 110 and call the police yourself.

酒店不方便帮您报警，因为事情的整个过程不是我们亲身经历的，一些细节我们无法和警察讲清，请您自己报警吧，号码是110。

193. And if there is anything more you need, please let us know.

如果还需要别的什么东西，请告诉我们。

194. Everything will be taken care of.

一切都会安排妥当的。

195. I will make a note of that.

我会把这件事记下来。

196. It's very kind of you.

你真是太客气了。

197. You are welcome./Not at all./Don't mention it.

不用谢。

198. It's my pleasure/with pleasure/my pleasure.

很高兴为您服务。

199. I'm always at your service.

可以为您效劳。

200. Thank you for staying in our hotel.

感谢您下榻我们酒店。

项目 2

The Housekeeping（客房部）

学习任务 1　Introducing Facilities（介绍酒店设施与服务）

工作任务	Introducing Facilities（介绍酒店设施与服务）	教学模式	线上线下混合教学模式 情境模拟教学模式
建议学时	2 学时	教学地点	智慧教室或多媒体教室
任务描述	行李员引领 Hanks 先生来到他的房间，在指引过程中客人对酒店的一些设施很感兴趣，行李员 John 为 Hanks 先生一一介绍；来到 Hanks 先生的门口，为 Hanks 先生打开门，帮助客人放好行李。Hanks 先生对房间的设施及物品摆设都非常满意，但是有一些设施和物品，他不知道怎样使用，John 为他仔细讲解		
学习目标	1. 掌握酒店设施及酒店客房设施相关的英文词汇。 2. 掌握介绍酒店常用设施的英文表达。 3. 能用英文介绍如何设置室内保险箱密码。 4. 能用方位词描述酒店各场所位置。 5. 能用英文简单介绍酒店周边著名旅游景点。 6. 通过训练，培养学生有效沟通的能力和敬业的工作素养		

头脑风暴

1. 酒店有哪些常用设施？用英文如何表达？
2. 酒店的客房都有哪些设备？用英文怎么说？
3. 如果你是行李员 John，如何给客人进行酒店内部及酒店房间设施的介绍？怎样给客人讲解房内设施——保险箱的使用和设置方法？

词汇储备

酒店内部设施

1. indoor swimming pool　室内游泳池
2. outdoor swimming pool　室外游泳池
3. fitness center　健身中心
4. bowling alley　保龄球场
5. billiard room　台球室
6. conference room　会议室（meeting room 规模较小）
7. coffee shop/Cafe　咖啡厅
8. business center　商务中心
9. Chinese restaurant　中餐厅
10. western restaurant　西餐厅
11. bar　酒吧
12. parking lot　停车场
13. gift shop　礼品店
14. leisure facility　休闲设施
15. lift（英式）/elevator（美式）电梯

房间设施

1. safe deposit box　保险箱
2. nice/good view　漂亮风景
3. channel　电视频道
4. air conditioner　空调
5. central air conditioning　中央空调
6. temperature control　（温度调节钮）
7. Internet access　互联网接入（上网）
8. Wi-Fi access　无线网络
9. luggage rack　行李架
10. remote control　遥控器
11. socket and switch　插座与开关

> 情境模拟

介绍酒店设施常用的句子：

1. Our hotel is a five-star hotel. There are 500 international standard-level guest rooms.

    我们是一家五星级酒店，有国际标准客房 500 间。

2. This is our hotel service brochure. It provides information regarding our hotel and services.

    这是我们酒店的服务手册，上面有关于我们酒店和服务的介绍信息。

3. Our Japanese restaurant is open every evening from 6 p.m. to 10 p.m.

    我们的日式餐厅的营业时间是晚 6 到 10 点。

4. Madam, our fitness center is on the 2nd floor and it's free of charge to use the sauna, indoor swimming pool and some healthy facilities on the fourth floor.

    女士，我们的健身中心在二楼，四楼的桑拿、室内游泳池和一些健身设施都是免费的。

5. We have three Chinese restaurants, one Western restaurant and one Italian restaurant and a bar.

    我们有三间中餐厅、一间西餐厅和一间意式餐厅，还有一个酒吧。

6. We have a nice gift shop on the first floor where you can buy some souvenirs.

    在一楼，有一间非常不错的礼品店，您在那儿能买到一些纪念品。

7. We have a 24-hour coffee shop on the first floor and five restaurants on different floors.

    一楼，我们有一家 24 小时营业的咖啡厅，在其他楼层还有五间餐厅。

8. All the rooms facing north have a nice garden view.

    所有朝北的房间都能观赏到花园的美景。

9. Take the elevator to the third floor and the fitness center is on your right.

    乘坐电梯到三楼，健身中心就在您的右手边。

10. The stairs/restrooms are around the corner over there.

    楼梯 / 洗手间在那边的转角附近。

介绍酒店设施与服务

情境 1：客人询问行李员索菲特酒店中餐厅的营业时间和位置。

　　G: Hello, when does the Chinese restaurant open?

　　B: It's open from 6 p.m. till 10.30 p.m.

　　G: Is it on the first floor?

　　B: No, it's on the third floor. Go out of the elevator and it is on your left.

情境 2：客人打来电话，想要了解一下酒店设施，接待员为客人一一介绍。

　　G: Could you tell me about your services before I make the reservation?

　　R: Sure, sir. We have three Chinese restaurants, two Western restaurants and

项目 2　The Housekeeping（客房部）

　　　　one Spanish restaurant and a cafe and a night bar. Our business center is fully equipped with everything you need. And there is a fitness center, an indoor swimming pool, a billiard room, a bowling alley and...

　　G: Are there any shopping facilities?

　　R: Yes, we have a nice gift shop...

　　G: That sounds great.

介绍房间设施常用的句子：

1. Sir/Madam, this is your room. Have a nice stay here!

　　先生/女士，这是您的房间。祝您入住愉快！

2. Your room faces Zhongshan park. It's a nice/lovely park. It takes only 10 minutes to walk there.

　　您的房间对面就是中山公园，公园特别漂亮，从这里步行到公园仅需 10 分钟。

3. This is our standard single room.

　　这是我们标准的单人间。

4. Here is the switch. This is the TV set and the remote control. We have 40 channels, including some foreign channels.

　　这是电灯开关。这是电视和遥控器，我们能观看 40 个频道，包括一些外文频道。

5. There are 20 channels for your choice. Here is the list of programs.

　　有 20 个频道供您选择，这是节目单。

6. The mini-bar is here. And there are many kinds of drinks at your choice.

　　这里是小冰箱。有许多种类的饮料供您选择。

7. This is the doorknob menu. The items are all on the menu.

　　这个是门把手菜单，所有的菜式都在这上面。

8. If you would like to have breakfast, mark the items down and hang it outside the door before you go to bed tonight.

　　如果您想用早餐，在菜单上标注，睡觉之前把菜单挂在外面即可。

9. If you want to keep your valuables, we have a safe deposit box in the closet.

　　如果您有贵重物品需要保管，可以放到柜子里的保险箱里。

10. This is the temperature control of the air-conditioner. You can turn it to adjust the temperature as you like.

　　这里是空调的温度控制钮，您可以随意调节您想要的温度。

情境 1：客人 Hanks 先生来到房间，刚进入，感觉有点热，于是他问行李员 John，空调的按钮在哪里，如何使用空调。

　　H: It is too hot in the room. Could you please turn on the air-conditioner?

　　J: Sure. Mr. Hanks.

43

H: And where is the button?

J: Here is the temperature control. And it is easy for you to adjust（调整）it by yourself. Just turn the control and you can turn it to adjust the temperature as you like.（turn it up or turn it down）

情境 2：Hanks 先生来到房间，问了有关电源电压的问题，他的电动剃须刀和国内使用的电压不一致，行李员 John 为 Hanks 先生一一解答。

H: My electric shaver operates at 110 volts. I am afraid it doesn't work here. What should I do?

J: The electrical current（电流）in your room is 220 volts. But don't worry. we have prepared transformers（变压器）to the guests. I'll bring you one at once.

能力进阶

想一想，再总结

介绍房间设施——告知客人如何使用酒店客房的电话拨打外线电话。常用的句子有：

1．Would you please show me how to use some of these devices (facilities)？（客人用语）

2．How can I make an outside call?（客人用语）

3．Please dial 9 first, and then dial the telephone number you want.

4．You may call directly from your room.

5．Please dial the country code, the area code and the number your want.

6．The country codes are listed in the services directory on the tea table.

7．For domestic calls（国内电话），please dial 0 first and then the area code and then the number you want.

介绍房间设施——告知客人如何使用酒店客房内的保险箱。常用的句子有：

1．Please open the safe.

2．When "open" is displayed（显示），you must set（设置）the code by inputting a six-digit password（六位密码）.

3．Then you need put the documents and valuables in it.

4．The safe will be locked when closed. At that time, "lock" will be displayed.

5．You must not forget the password you set, otherwise it will cause a lot of trouble.

6．If you put in the wrong number, it will show "Error" and will not open.

7．You have to remember the password that you set.

语言使用

方位介词的使用

1．into / out of...

　　进……里面 / 出……外面

You can go into the guest room.

走进房间

Please walk out of the elevator.

走出电梯

2. at the top of...

   在……顶部

   at the bottom of...

   在……底部

   The swimming pool is at the top of the hotel.

   游泳池在酒店顶层。

   The parking lot is at the bottom of the building.

   停车场在这幢楼的底层。

3. across from

   在……对面

   next to

   紧挨着……

   The fitness center is next to the billiard room.

   紧挨着台球室。

   The bowling alley is across from the fitness center.

   保龄球馆在健身中心对面。

4. in front of（无范围）/in the front of

   在……前面（物体内部前面）

   The reception desk is in the front of the lobby.

   前台在大厅前面。

   The shopping mall is in front of the hotel.

   商场在宾馆前面。

5. along

   沿着

   through

   穿过（从物体内部穿过）

   Go along the corridor and you will see the Chinese restaurant.

   沿着走廊走，您就会看到中餐厅。

   Go through the Chinese restaurant, you will see the cafe.

   穿过中餐厅，您就会看到咖啡厅。

6. get on+ 交通工具（上……）/get off+ 交通工具（下……）

   Get on the subway at Zhongshan Park stop.

   在中山公园站上地铁。

Get off the bus at Sofitel Hotel stop.
在索菲特酒店站下车。

7. in the end of...
在……的尽头
The restroom is in the end of the corridor.
洗手间在走廊尽头。

8. on the (your) right
在您的右边
on the (your) left
在您的左边
The elevator is just on your right.
电梯就在您的右边。
You will see the gift shop and it's on your left.
它在您的左边。

9. on the first floor
在一层
on the top floor
在顶层
The swimming pool is on the top floor.
游泳池在顶层。
The business center is on the first floor.
商务中心在一层。

能力训练

情境 1：

行李员 John 引领 Hanks 先生来到他的房间，在指引过程中，Hanks 先生对酒店的一些设施很感兴趣，行李员 John 为他一一介绍。

The bellboy, John, shows the way for the guest, Hanks, and introduces some hotel facilities and service to Hanks, including eating, drinking, leisure and so on.

要求：两人一组，完成对话，注意服务礼仪及方位介词。

情境 2：

来到 Hanks 先生的门口，行李员 John 为 Hanks 先生打开门，帮助他放好行李。Hanks 先生对房间的设施及物品摆设都非常满意，但是他不知道怎样调试空调温度和拨打国际长途，John 为他仔细讲解。

要求：两人一组，完成对话，注意服务礼仪。

学习任务 2　Room Cleaning Service（客房清扫服务）

工作任务	Room Cleaning Service（客房清扫服务）	教学模式	线上线下混合教学模式 情境模拟教学模式
建议学时	4学时	教学地点	智慧教室或多媒体教室
任务描述	Tom Hanks 先生等一行七人入住沈阳丽都索菲特酒店后，对酒店提供的接待、餐饮及商务服务都非常满意。在酒店，"住"是根本，接下来，酒店会让 Hanks 先生等人感受到宾至如归的感觉，体验酒店客房部提供的各种服务		
学习目标	1. 掌握客房设施和客房清扫相关的英文词汇。 2. 掌握客房清扫服务程序及各个程序的英文表达。 3. 当客人不方便此时打扫时，能够用英文与客人沟通合适的时间。 4. 能用英文询问客人有无其他需求，并满足客人需求。 5. 通过学习任务，培养学生热爱劳动的情怀		

头脑风暴

1. 酒店客房部的工作任务有哪些？最基本的是哪一项？
2. 酒店的客房都有哪些房间设施？用英文怎么说？
3. 如果你是酒店客房服务员，给客人进行客房清扫的服务程序是什么，各个程序应如何与客人进行英语沟通？
4. 如果客人不方便打扫，怎么用英语与客人沟通？

词汇储备

客房

1. curtain　窗帘　draw the curtains　拉上窗帘
2. closet　壁柜（wardrobe 大衣柜）
3. table lamp　台灯　stand lamp　落地灯
4. bedside cupboard　床头柜
5. sewing kit　针线包
6. price list　价目表
7. drawer　抽屉
8. slipper　拖鞋
9. ashtray　烟灰缸

10. washing basin   洗手盆

11. towel set   毛巾架   face towel   面巾   bath towel   浴巾

12. bath mat   地巾

13. bathtub   浴缸   bathrobe   浴衣   bath foam   浴液

14. shampoo   洗发水   soap   香皂

15. toothpaste   牙膏   toothbrush   牙刷

16. toilet   马桶   toilet paper   卷纸   water tank   水箱

17. quilt   被子   quilt cover   被罩

18. pillowcase   枕套   pillow   枕头

19. sheet   床单（100% cotton）

20. mattress   床垫

21. blanket   毯子   carpet   地毯

22. baby cot   婴儿床

23. rug   地毯

打扫服务

1. make up the room   整理房间

2. do the room   打扫房间

3. clean the room   打扫房间

4. tidy up the room   打扫整理房间

5. convenient   *a.* 方便的

6. DND sign= do not disturb   请勿打扰

房况 Room Status

1. 入住房：又称 OCC 房。客人已入住。

Occupied: The room is registered to a current guest.

2. 待售房：又称 VC 房。干净可以随时出租的房间。

Vacant and Clean: The room has been cleaned and is ready for use.

3. 空脏房：又称 VD 房。空房但是没有收拾干净，无法出租。

Vacant and Dirty: The room hasn't been cleaned and isn't ready for use.

4. 故障房：又称 OOO 房。房间内的一些设施出了故障，不能出售。

Out of order: There is something wrong with the facilities in the room and it can't be sold.

5. 外宿房：又称 SO 房。客人没有回来住，为干净房（没有动过卫生间及床铺）。

Sleep-out: The room is reported as occupied, but the room was not used and the guest is not present.

6. 请勿打扰房：又称 DND 房。客人在门上挂上"请勿打扰"的标志。

DND means do not disturb. The guest hangs the sign on the door for not being disturbed.

7. 请即打扫房：又称 MUR 房。

MUR means make up room now.

项目 2　The Housekeeping（客房部）

服务流程

客房清扫服务

客房清扫服务（情况一）流程如下：

1. Asking the guest if I can go into the room.
   询问客人是否可以进房间。
2. Greetings and asking the guest if I can clean the room now.
   问候并询问客人是否可以现在打扫。
3. Cleaning and asking the guest if he has some other requests when it is done.
   打扫完毕后，询问客人是否还有其他事宜。
4. Expressing the wishes.
   表达祝愿。

客房清扫服务（情况二）流程如下：

1. Asking the guest if I can go into the room.
   询问客人是否可以进房间。
2. Greetings and asking the guest if I can make the room now.
   问候并询问客人是否可以现在打扫。
3. Asking the guest a better time.
   和客人商量一个合适的时间（再来打扫）。
4. Expressing the wishes.
   表达祝愿。

情境模拟

客房清扫服务（情况一）流程及句子表达如下：

1. The first step: Asking the guest if I can go into the room.
   第一步：询问客人是否可以进房间。常用的句子有：
   a. Housekeeping, may I come in?
      客房部，我可以进来吗？
   b. Good morning/afternoon, housekeeping, may I come through?
      早上好 / 下午好，客房部，我可以进来吗？
   c. Good morning, room-cleaning service, may I come in?
      早上好，客房清扫服务，我能进来吗？

情境 1：客房服务员来到房门外，准备进入为其打扫房间。
　　　　　Good morning, Housekeeping, may I come in?

情境 2：下午，客房服务员来到客人 Hanks 先生房门外，准备进入为其打扫房间。
　　　　　Housekeeping, Mr.Hanks, may I come through?

49

2. The second step: Greetings and asking the guest if I can clean the room now.
   第二步：询问客人是否可以进房间。常用的句子有：

   a. Good morning/ afternoon, may I do/clean the room now?
      早上好 / 下午好，我现在能为您打扫房间吗？

   b. Good morning/ afternoon, may I make up the room now?
      早上好 / 下午好，我现在能为您整理房间吗？

   c. Good afternoon, sir. I am here for the housekeeping. May I clean the room now?
      下午好，先生。我来整理房间，现在可以打扫吗？

   d. (I am) Sorry to disturb you, but may I do your room now?
      很抱歉打扰您，现在能为您打扫房间吗？

   e. I hope I haven't disturbed you, but may I clean your room now?
      希望没有打扰到您，现在能为您打扫房间吗？

   f. Sorry to have taken up your time, I'd like to clean the room. May I do it now?
      抱歉占用了您的时间，我想为您打扫房间，现在可以吗？

   g. Would you mind me cleaning /making up /your room now?
      您介意我现在给您打扫房间吗？

   h. Would you like me to clean/make up/do your room now?
      您想让我现在给您打扫房间吗？

情境 1：客房服务员进入房间，询问客人是否可以现在打扫。
   Good morning, madam, may I do/clean the room now?

情境 2：客房服务员进入 Hanks 先生的房间，Hanks 先生正在工作，询问其是否可以现在打扫房间。
   Sorry to disturb you, Mr. Hanks, but may I do your room now?

情境 3：客房服务员进入房间，询问客人是否可以打扫客房。
   Good morning, madam. I'm here for the housekeeping. May I clean the room now?

3. The third step: Cleaning and asking the guest if he has some other request when it is done.
   第三步：打扫完毕后，询问客人是否还有其他事宜。常用的句子有：

   a. I've finished cleaning the room. (Is there) anything else I can do for you?
      房间已经打扫完了，还有什么我能为您做的吗？

   b. I've finished cleaning the room. What else do you want?/ What else would you like?
      房间已经打扫完了，还有什么事情吗？

   c. Your room is made up, madam. Anything else I can do for you?
      女士，您的房间整理好了，还有什么我能为您做的吗？

情境 1：客房服务员为客人整理完房间，准备离开。

项目 2　The Housekeeping（客房部）

I've finished cleaning the room. Anything else I can do for you?

情境 2： 客房服务员按照 Hanks 先生的要求整理完房间，准备离开。

Sir, your room is made up. Anything else I can do for you?

4. The fourth step: Expressing the wishes.
   第四步：表达祝愿。常用的句子有：

   a. (I) hope you'll have a nice day.
      祝您一天时光愉快。

   b. I am glad to be of your service.
      乐意为您效劳。

   c. Please contact us if you need any help.
      如有需要，请与我们联系。

   d. Please don't hesitate to let me know if you need any help.
      如果您需要任何帮助，请不要犹豫与我们联系。

情境 1： 离开客人 Smith 先生房间时，祝福客人。

Mr. Smith, hope you'll have a nice day.

情境 2： 离开客人房间时，告知客人有事情一定要联系客房部。

Madam, please don't hesitate to let us know if you need any help.

客房清扫服务（情况二）流程及句子表达如下：

1. The first step: Asking the guest if I can go into the room.
   第一步：询问客人是否可以进房间。

2. The second step: Greetings and asking the guest if I can clean the room now.
   第二步：询问客人是否可以打扫房间。

3. The third step: Asking the guest a better/convenient time.
   第三步：和客人商量一个最佳/合适的时间（再来打扫）。

   a. When would you like me to clean your room?
      您想让我什么时候来打扫？

   b. Sir, what time would it be better for you?
      先生，您什么时候方便我来打扫？

   c. Madam, when would it be convenient for you?
      女士，您什么时候方便我来打扫？

   d. Shall I come back later, sir?
      我晚点再来，先生，行吗？

   e. What time /When would you like me to come back?
      您希望我什么时候回来给您打扫？

51

f. You can call the housekeeping dept, when you want your room done.
如果您想要打扫房间，请给客房部打电话。

g. Just let us know if you want your room cleaned earlier.
如果您想早点打扫房间，尽管让我们知道。

4. The fourth step: Expressing the wishes.
第四步：表达祝愿。

情境 1： 客房服务员要为客人打扫房间，但客人此时有点忙。

G: I am a little busy now.

R: Sir, what time would it be better for you?

G: What about an hour later?

R: OK. I will come back in one hour.

情境 2： 客房服务员要为客人 Hanks 先生打扫房间，但客人此时想要休息，不方便打扫。

G: I would like to have a rest after the work.

R: You may have a hot bath. It is good for you to relax.

G: Thank you so much.

R: Sir, when would it be convenient for you to clean your room?

G: No, not today.

R: That's OK. Have a good rest.

能力进阶

在打扫房间过程中，客人有其他需求，服务程序及常用的句子有：

1. The first step: Asking the guest if I can go into the room.
   第一步：询问客人是否可以进房间。

2. The second step: Greetings and asking the guest if I can clean the room now.
   第二步：询问客人是否可以打扫房间。

3. The third step: Cleaning and meeting the guest's needs.
   第三步：打扫房间并满足客人需求。

   A: Could you tidy up the bathroom first? It is quite a mess now.
   能先打扫卫生间吗？卫生间现在太乱了。

   B: Of course, sir. I will clean the bathroom right now.
   当然可以，先生。我马上打扫卫生间。

   A: Could you bring me some...?
   能给我拿一些……？

   B: No problem, madam. I will bring... after I finish cleaning.
   没问题，女士。我打扫完就给您拿……

项目 2　The Housekeeping（客房部）

A: I feel cold at night. Could you give me another blanket?

晚上特别冷，能再给我那一条毯子吗？

B: Sure. I will bring one after I finish cleaning.

当然可以。我打扫完就给您拿一条。

A: The rug might have given me some problems. I kept sneezing. I have sensitive allergy.

地毯给我带来一些困扰，我不停地打喷嚏。我有鼻子敏感过敏症。

B: Sorry, madam. We will remove the rug at once.

抱歉，女士。我们立刻给您更换。

4. The fourth step: Expressing the wishes.

第四步：表达祝愿。

语言使用

some 和 any 的用法

1. some "一些"，用于肯定句和疑问句。

（1）some 用于肯定句。

a. I want some extra pillows.

我想再要些枕头。

b. I'd like to order some drinks.

我想要点些饮料。

c. I prefer to have some tea, please.

我想喝茶。

（2）some 用于疑问句，表示向对方主动提供某物或要求某物并期望得到对方的肯定回答。

a. Can I have some extra pillows?

能给我再拿几个枕头吗？

b. What about some cotton sheets?

你们有纯棉的床单吗？

c. Would you like some orange juice?

来点橙汁怎么样？

2. any "一些"，常用于否定和疑问句中。

（1）Do you have any special requests?

您有什么特殊需求吗？

（2）Are there any nice shopping malls near here?

这附近有什么好的购物中心吗？

（3）I will not drink any tea today.

我今天不喝茶。

（4）I am afraid we don't have any newspapers today.
恐怕今天没有报纸。

3．练一练

（1）Would you like to have _____ more tea, sir?

（2）Do you mind bringing me _____ more blankets, please?

（3）I can't eat _____ cream cakes because I am on a diet at the moment.

（4）We could order _____ buns with our coffee.

（5）I am afraid we don't offer _____ Irish whiskey.

能力训练

情境 1：

服务员来到 Hanks 先生的房间，准备打扫，但是 Hanks 先生由于有一个重要的电话要接听，暂时不方便打扫。与客人用英文进行沟通商量一个合适的时间。

要求：两人一组，完成对话。

情境 2：

客房服务员到 Miller 女士的房间为其打扫，但是 Miller 女士要求服务员先打扫一下浴室，她刚刚洗完澡有点乱，房间其他地方另约时间打扫（Miller 有公务要处理），同时 Miller 要求帮助她把空调温度调低一些，还询问如何收看英文电视节目。

单词提示：air conditioner, television, remote control, turn down, adjust

要求：两人一组，完成对话，注意服务礼仪。

学习任务 3 Laundry Service（洗衣服务）

工作任务	Laundry Service（洗衣服务）	教学模式	线上线下混合教学模式 情境模拟教学模式
建议学时	4 学时	教学地点	智慧教室或多媒体教室
任务描述	Hanks 先生周三晚上要参加一个晚宴，需要正装出席，他向客房服务员询问客房部是否提供洗衣服务及有关洗衣服务的一些事宜		
学习目标	1. 掌握有关洗衣服务的英文词汇。 2. 掌握洗衣服务的服务程序及各个程序里常用的英文语句。 3. 能用英文流利地向客人解释 express service 和 regular service 的区别。 4. 能够听懂客人关于洗衣的特殊需求，并能够用英文向客人解释有关 laundry service 事宜（收费、时间、损坏、设备等）。 5. 能看懂客人填写的洗衣单并会填写洗衣单。 6. 通过学习任务，培养学生有效的沟通能力和优秀的职业道德		

头脑风暴

1. 各种衣物的英文表达，你会说吗？
2. 如果你是客房服务员，如何受理 Hanks 先生的洗衣请求呢？服务程序是什么？需要从 Hanks 先生那里获知哪些信息？
3. 如何为客人用英文介绍酒店的洗衣服务？快洗服务和普通洗服务都是酒店客房部提供的洗衣服务，该如何用英文解释区别？

词汇储备

洗衣项目

1. laundry   n. 要洗的衣服
2. laundry supervisor   洗衣主管
3. laundryman   洗衣工
4. room attendant & housemaid   客房服务员
5. laundry list/form   洗衣单
6. laundry bag   洗衣袋
7. laundry charge/fee   洗衣费用
8. laundry damage   洗衣损坏

9. laundry indemnity   洗衣赔偿

10. laundry drier   烘干机

11. express service   快洗服务

12. same day   当日取

13. next day   次日取

14. regular service   正常洗服务

15. professional equipment   专业设备

16. washing   *n.* 洗，水洗

17. dry cleaning   干洗

18. ironing   *n.* 熨烫

19. dyeing   *n.* 上色

20. starch   *v.* 上浆

21. shrink   *v.* 缩水

22. fade   *v.* 褪色

23. stitch   *v.* 缝缀 (stitch the buttons)

24. stain   *n.* 污点

25. item   *n.* 衣服的件

服装类

1. blouse   女衬衫

2. dress   连衣裙

3. skirt   短裙

4. scarf   围巾

5. socks   短袜

6. stockings   长袜

7. sweater   毛衣

8. trousers   西裤

9. shorts   短裤

10. tie   领带

11. jacket   夹克

12. T-shirt   T恤衫

13. vest   背心

14. gloves   手套

服务流程

洗衣服务流程如下：

1. Greetings.
   问候。

洗衣服务

2. Collecting the laundry.
   收取客人要洗的衣服。
3. Asking the guest's request.
   了解客人的洗衣需求。
4. Telling the guest to fill in the laundry list.
   告知客人填写洗衣单。
5. Expressing the wishes.
   表达祝愿。

情境模拟

1. The first step: Greetings.
   第一步：问候。常用的句子有：
   a. Good morning, housekeeping, may I come in?
      早上好，客房部，我可以进来吗？
   b. Good afternoon, laundry service, may I come through?
      下午好，洗衣服务，我能进来吗？
   c. Could you send someone up for my laundry, please?（客人）
      能派个人上来收一下我要洗的衣物吗？

   情境 1： 客房服务员来到的房门外，准备进入收取客人要洗的衣服。
   Good morning, housekeeping, may I come in?

   情境 2： 下午，客房服务员来到客人 Hanks 先生房门外，准备进入收取客人要洗的衣服。
   Housekeeping, Mr.Hanks, may I come through?

2. The second step: Collecting the laundry.
   第二步：收取客人要洗的衣服。常用的句子有：
   a. Good morning, madam, I'm here to collect your laundry.
      早上好，女士，我来收您要洗的衣物。
   b. Excuse me, have you got any laundry/do you have any laundry?
      打扰一下，您有要洗的衣服吗？
   c. Excuse me, the laundry man is here to collect your laundry.
      打扰一下，洗衣部的员工来这收取您要洗的衣物。

   情境 1： 客房服务员进入房间，收取 Miller 女士要洗的衣物。
   Good morning, Miss Miller, I'm here to collect your laundry.

   情境 2： 洗衣部员工敲门进入客房后，询问客人是否有要洗的衣物。
   Excuse me, sir, have you got any laundry?

3. The third step: Asking the guest's request.
   第三步：了解客人的洗衣需求。常用的句子有：

   a. If you have any, please just leave it in the laundry bag.
      如果您有要洗的衣物，请您放到洗衣袋里。

   b. Please tell us or notify in the laundry list whether you need your clothes ironed, mended...
      请您告诉我们或在洗衣单上注明，您是想要熨烫、缝补……

   c. Do you have any special requests for your laundry?
      您对要洗的衣物有什么特殊需求吗？

   d. When would you like to get them back?
      您希望什么时候取回您的衣物？

   e. We will deliver them tomorrow evening...
      我们会明天晚上给您送回。

   f. Would you like express service or same day?
      您想用快洗服务还是普通洗服务？

情境 1：Miller 女士想让她的羊毛衫冷水手洗，告知客人注明在洗衣单上。
G: I would like this sweater to be washed by hand in cold water, for it might shrink.
L: I see, madam. But please notify it in the laundry list.

情境 2：收取衣物时，客人没有要洗的衣物，告知客人一些洗衣事宜。
G: I don't have any laundry now.
L: If you have any, please just leave it in the laundry bag. And tell us whether you need your clothes ironed, mended or dry cleaned.

情境 3：询问客人对于衣物有何特殊要求。
Madam, do you have any special requests for your laundry?

4. The fourth step: Telling the guest to fill in the laundry list.
   第四步：告知客人填写洗衣单。常用的句子有：

   a. Would you please fill in the laundry list?
      您能填写一下洗衣单吗？

   b. Would you mind filling in /out the laundry list?
      您介意填写一下洗衣单吗？

   c. Would you like to fill in /out the laundry list?
      您能填写一下洗衣单吗？

   d. Please fill out the laundry list.
      请填写一下洗衣单。

   e. Could you fill out the laundry list?
      您能填写一下洗衣单吗？

情境 1：告知 Miller 女士填写洗衣单。

　　Miss. Miller, would you please fill in the laundry list?

情境 2：告知客人填写洗衣单。

　　Sir, would you mind filling out the laundry form?

5. The fifth step: Expressing the wishes.

　　第五步：表达祝愿。常用的句子有：

　　a. Glad to be of your service.
　　　愿意为您效劳。

　　b. Certainly, madam. I'm glad to help.
　　　当然可以，女士。荣幸之至。

　　c. If there is anything we can do for you, just let us know.
　　　如果有需要，随时联系我们。

情境 1：离开客人 Miller 女士的房间时，祝福客人。

　　Miss Miller, hope you'll have a nice day.

情境 2：离开客人房间时，告知客人有事情一定要联系客房部。

　　Madam, if there is anything we can do for you, just let us know.

能力进阶

客人 Hanks 先生想要了解有关洗衣服务事宜，解释洗衣服务常用的句子有：

快洗服务与普通洗服务

1. 如果您想了解更进一步的信息，请参照洗衣单。

　　Please refer to the laundry list for further information.

2. 对普通洗的衣物，早上 11 点前收取，我们同一天晚上 9 点前送还给您，下午 3 点前收取的，第二天中午之前送还。

　　For clothes received before 11:00 a.m., we'll deliver them to your room by 9:00 p.m. the same day; And for those received before 3:00 p.m., you may get them back by noon the next day.

3. 快洗服务 3 个小时之内送还给你，但是要加收 50% 的服务费。

　　For express service, we deliver the laundry within 3 hours, but we add 50% service charge.

4. 普通洗，我们有当日取和次日取；快洗，有快洗和快熨服务。

　　For regular service, we have sameday service and for express service, we have express and express pressing service.

5. 如果洗衣有损坏，我们会赔偿，但费用不会超过洗衣费用的 10 倍。

　　We should certainly pay for the laundry damage, but the laundry indemnity will not exceed ten times of the laundry charge.

6. 我们的员工很有经验并且也有专业的设备。

The staff in the laundry department are experienced and we also have the professional equipments.

解释普通洗与快洗服务，常用的句子有：

1. We have regular service and express service for the laundry.
2. Regular service is usually made up of the same day service and the next day service.
3. It often takes one or two days for the regular service.
4. The express service often takes three or four hours.
5. The laundry can be collected all day and returned within 4 hours for the express service.
6. We also charge 50% more for the express service.
7. We charge 50% more for the express service, but it only takes four hours.
8. We have the express pressing service.
9. It only takes 1 hour to press any laundry for the express pressing service.
10. For the express service, it is quicker but with a 50% service charge.
11. For the express service, it is faster but with a 50% extra charge.
12. Would you like the express service or the regular service?
13. We have a two-hour express service with an extra charge of 50%.
14. If you choose the express pressing, we will press it within 40 minutes.

语言使用

英文中的数字表达法（一）

1. 英文中年份的读法。

（1）表示年份的四个数字分成两组，每两个数字一组，按照基数词来读。

1993 年：nineteen ninety-three　　1987 年：nineteen eighty-seven

（2）关于千年的读法。

2000 年：two thousand

2008 年：two thousand and eight 或 twenty O eight

2019 年：two thousand and nineteen 或 twenty nineteen

2021 年：two thousand and twenty-one 或 twenty twenty-one

2. 英文中月份的读法。

书写时，可以用缩写（前三个字母，注意首字母要大写，后面加 .，如 Mar., Oct.。）

一月：January	二月：February	三月：March
四月：April	五月：May	六月：June
七月：July	八月：August	九月：September
十月：October	十一月：November	十二月：December

3. 英文中日期的读法。

英文的日子要用序数词表达，可用缩写 1st, 2nd, 3rd, 4th, 15th, 21st。

一日：First　　二日：second　　三日：third　　四日：fourth
十五日：fifth　　二十日：twentieth　　二十一日：twenty first

4．英文中年月日的读法。

可以按照日月年的顺序（英式），也可以按照月日年的顺序（美式）。

2019 年 4 月 6 日，写作：6th April，2019

读作：(the) sixth April, twenty nineteen

也可写作：April 6th，2019

读作：April (the) sixth, twenty nineteen

2020 年 11 月 22 日，写作：22nd Nov.，2020

读作：(the) twenty second November, two thousand and twenty

也可写作：November 22nd，2020

读作：November the twenty second, two thousand and twenty

能力训练

情境 1：

上午 9 点，客房服务员来到 Miller 女士的房间外，准备敲门进入收取 Miller 女士要洗的 dress，并得到允许。

要求：两人一组，完成对话，注意服务礼仪。

情境 2：

客房服务员来到 Hanks 先生的房间提供洗衣服务，但是 Hanks 先生此时没有要洗的衣服。他问了几个有关洗衣服务的问题（关于洗衣损坏、洗衣收费等），服务员听懂了 Hanks 先生的问题，并一一作答。

要求：两人一组，完成对话，注意服务礼仪。

情境 3：

Green 女士给酒店房务中心打来电话要求为她洗一件丝绸连衣裙，她不知道连衣裙是否缩水，另外，Green 女士还需要为她的丈夫 Jacket 先生缝补一下再清洗。Green 女士最终选择了快洗服务。

要求：两人一组，完成对话，注意服务礼仪。

学习任务 4　Ordering Room Service（客房订餐服务）

工作任务	Ordering Room Service（客房订餐服务）	教学模式	线上线下混合教学模式 情境模拟教学模式
建议学时	4 学时	教学地点	智慧教室或多媒体教室
任务描述	Hanks 先生等人明天早上要参加一个非常重要的商务会议，他们没有时间到餐厅就餐，于是他们决定尝试一下酒店的 Room Service 服务，Hanks 先生拿起了电话，打给送餐部，要求预订明早的早餐		
学习目标	1. 掌握外国早餐的分类；American breakfast 和 Continental breakfast 都包含哪些食物。 2. 掌握电话客房订餐（当面订餐）的服务程序及各个程序里常用的英文语句。 3. 能够流利地用英文解释什么是门把手菜单（doorknob menu）。 4. 能听懂客人关于客房订/送餐的投诉，能用英语向客人解释原因和致歉。 5. 培养学生发现问题、分析问题及解决问题的能力		

头脑风暴

1. 什么是 room service?
2. 客房订餐的类型有哪些？什么是 doorknob menu?
3. 酒店的 room service 可以提供早餐、午餐和正餐，常见的早餐的类型有哪些？能符合 Hanks 先生等人的口味吗？
4. 如果你是酒店客房服务员，如何给客人通过电话或当面订餐呢？应遵循什么程序？各个程序应如何与客人进行英语沟通，其中哪个程序更重要一些？

词汇储备

词汇 Vocabulary

1. Room service　客房服务
2. Room service menu　客房服务菜单
3. DND sign (Do Not Disturb)　请勿打扰
4. doorknob menu　门把手菜单
5. order　*v.* 点餐
6. hang　*v.* 挂在
7. snack　*n.* 零食，小吃
8. mark down　记下，写下
9. breakfast　*n.* 早餐

10. Chinese breakfast 中式早餐
11. lunch *n.* 午餐
12. dinner *n.* 晚餐（正餐）
13. light *a.* 清淡的
14. heavy *a.* 口味重的

早餐 Breakfast

1. Continental breakfast 欧式早餐

    （1）Fruit or juice 水果或果汁

    canned juice 罐装果汁　fresh juice 新鲜果汁

    grapefruit juice 西柚汁

    tomato juice 番茄汁

    orange juice 橙汁

    pineapple juice 菠萝汁

    grape juice 葡萄汁

    strawberry juice 草莓汁

    mango juice 芒果汁

    mixed vegetable juice 什锦蔬菜汁

    （2）Cereals 谷物

    corn flakes 玉米片

    oatmeal 燕麦片

    （3）Toast and Bread 吐司和面包

    toast 吐司

    bread 面包

    toast with butter 是指吐司和牛油是分开的

    buttered toast 是指把牛油涂在吐司上面

    corn bread 玉米面包

    biscuit 饼干

    croissant 牛角面包

    doughnut 甜甜圈

    （4）Beverages 咖啡或茶等不含酒精的饮料

    white coffee 加牛奶（milk）或奶油（cream）的咖啡

    black coffee 不加牛奶或奶油的咖啡

    black tea 红茶（早餐一般饮用红茶）

    green tea 绿茶（早餐较少）

2. American breakfast 美式早餐

    美式早餐与欧陆式早餐相同的项目：

    juice, corn flakes, toast and butter, tea or coffee

不同项目：

(1) Sausage 香肠

(2) Eggs 鸡蛋

fried egg 煎荷包蛋类

sunny-side up 单面煎（蛋黄在上）

sunny-side down 单面煎（蛋黄在下）

over easy 双面煎（不熟）

over hard 双面煎（熟）

boiled egg 水煮蛋类

soft boiled egg 水煮蛋（嫩）

hard boiled egg 水煮蛋（老）

scrambled egg 炒鸡蛋

omelet 蛋卷

(3) Bacon 培根

(4) Beans 豆类

3. Chinese breakfast 中式早餐

Chinese congee (with beef, pork, chicken, preserved egg) 粤式粥类（可搭配牛肉、猪肉、鸡肉或皮蛋）

millet gruel 小米粥

fried noodles 炒面

bread 面包

pickled vegetables 泡菜

Chinese tea 中国茶

dumpling 饺子

stretched noodles 拉面

sweet dumpling 汤圆

wonton 馄饨

meat pie 馅饼

rice noodles 米粉

4. Dinner 西式正餐

steak 牛排

salad 沙拉

vegetable salad 蔬菜沙拉

fruit salad 水果沙拉

mixed salad 混合沙拉

dressing 调味料（配沙拉用）

French dressing 法式味汁

项目 2　The Housekeeping（客房部）

Thousand Island　千岛酱
beef steak　牛排
lamb steak　羊排
blue rare　近生牛排
rare　一分熟（R）
medium rare　三分熟（MR）
medium　五分熟（M）
medium well　七分熟（MW）
well done　全熟（WD）

服务流程

客房订餐服务流程（电话与当面）如下：

1. Greetings.
   问候。

2. Getting information from the guest.
   获取客人订餐信息。

   a. What does the guest want?
      客人要吃什么？

   b. The special demands for cooking.
      烹饪需求。

   c. Guest's name and room number.
      客人姓名和房号。

3. Confirming what the guest ordered.
   确认客人所点菜肴。

4. Expressing the wishes.
   表达祝愿。

客房订餐服务

情境模拟

客房订餐服务流程及句子表达如下：

1. The first step: Greetings.
   第一步：问候。常用的句子有：

   a. Good morning/afternoon, room service, what can I do for you?
      （当面或电话）
      早上好，客房服务，有什么能帮到您的？

   b. Good evening, Mr. Hanks. How may I help you?（当面）
      晚上好，Hanks 先生。我能帮到您吗？

情境 1：上午 8 点，订餐部服务员接到 VIP Smith 先生的预订 room service 电话。
Good morning, Mr. Smith, how may I help you?

情境 2：下午，订餐部服务员接到了预订明早 room service 客人的电话。
Good afternoon, Room service, May I help you?

2. The second step: Getting information from the guest.
第二步：获取客人订餐信息。常用的句子有：

    a. We offer three types of breakfast: American breakfast, Continental breakfast and Chinese breakfast. Which one would you like?
       我们提供三种早餐供您选择，有美式、欧式和中式，您想吃哪一种？

    b. Which breakfast would you prefer? American or Continental?
       您想吃哪种早餐，美式还是欧式？

    c. What kind of juice would you like, strawberry or orange?
       您想喝哪种果汁，草莓汁还是橙汁？

    d. Would you like ham or bacon with your eggs?
       你想点火腿还是培根搭配您的鸡蛋？

    e. Would you like rolls or toast?
       您想吃面包圈还是吐司？

    f. How would you like your eggs?
       您点的鸡蛋，您打算怎么做？（如何烹饪）

    g. How would you like your steak?
       您想要几分熟的牛排？

    h. What's your special request for cooking?
       您对烹饪有什么特殊需求吗？

    i. May I know your special request for cooking?
       您能告诉我您对烹饪的特殊需求吗？

    j. What time/when would you like your breakfast?
       What time would you like to have your breakfast?
       您打算什么时间吃？

    k. Will there be anything else, Mr. Hanks?
       Hanks 先生，还有什么其他需要吗？

    l. May I know/have your name and room number?
       您的名字和房号是多少？

情境 1：客人 Hanks 先生询问早餐分类，服务员告知。
Sir, We offer three types of breakfast: American breakfast, Continental breakfast and Chinese breakfast. Which one would you like/prefer?

项目 2　The Housekeeping（客房部）

情境 2：客人点了欧式早餐和两个煎蛋。
　　　　Madam, how would you like your fried eggs?
情境 3：客人不知道喝什么果汁，向客人推荐。
　　　　Sir, we have a good choice of juice, mango, orange, grape, watermelon and they are all fresh now. Which one would you like?
情境 4：客人点了炒蛋，但没点肉类，如香肠或培根。
　　　　Madam, would you like ham or bacon with your scrambled eggs and what about some beans?
情境 5：VIP Smith 先生订完餐后，询问客人的房间号。
　　　　Mr. Smith, may I have your room number?
情境 6：客人点完了早餐，询问客人想要什么时间用餐。
　　　　Madam, what time would you like to have your breakfast?

3. The third step: Confirming what the guest ordered.
　 第三步：确认客人所点菜肴。常用的句子有：
   a. Let me confirm your order... Is that right/correct?
      让我为您确认一下订单，您点了……对吗？
   b. May/could I just read that back to you, sir/madam?
      女士 / 先生，我能为您确认一下您的订单吗？
   c. I will just confirm it to you, sir/madam. That is...
      先生 / 女士，我给您确认下订单，有……
   d. I will repeat your order...
      我为您重复一下菜单……
   e. So your order is...
      您点了……
   f. So...
      您点了……

情境 1：和客人确认信息，客人点了两份欧式早餐，配橙汁，一份配咖啡，一份配柠檬茶，两份早餐都要了牛角面包。
　　　　Sir, let me confirm your order, two Continental breakfast with orange juice, one with coffee, one with lemon tea. Croissants for both. Is that right?
情境 2：和客人确认信息，客人点了一份中式早餐、一份美式早餐，配一个蛋黄向上的单面煎鸡蛋、培根、番茄豆和一杯咖啡？
　　　　Madam, I will just confirm it to you, you ordered a Chinese breakfast, an American breakfast, bacon with a fried egg, sunny side up and beans and a cup of coffee, am I right?
情境 3：客人 Hanks 先生点了三份中式早餐、两份中式炒面、一份皮蛋瘦肉粥、两杯中国茶和两份千岛酱蔬菜沙拉。

Mr. Hanks, I will repeat your order. You have three Chinese breakfast, a Chinese congee with preserved eggs, two Chinese tea and two mixed vegetable salad with Thousand Island, is that correct?

4. The fourth step: Expressing the wishes.
   第四步：表达祝愿。常用的句子有：

   a. It should be (here) with you in 20 minutes, sir.
      您点的餐 20 分钟就好。

   b. It should be ready in about an hour, madam.
      您的餐 1 小时能做好。

   c. You should/can get it in about 30 minutes.
      您点的餐 30 分钟就好。

   d. Thank you for your calling. Have a nice day！
      感谢您的来电，祝您一天愉快！

   e. Thank you for your calling and your breakfast will be ready in 15 minutes.
      感谢您的来电，您的早餐 15 分钟就好。

情境 1：告知客人，早餐半小时后就好。
   Sir, you should get your breakfast in about 30 minutes.

情境 2：告知客人，中式早餐 20 分钟就好，感谢他的来电。
   Sir, thank you for your calling. It should be (here) with you in 20 minutes. Have a nice day.

能力进阶

客房订餐的常用句子：

1. There is a room service menu in the middle drawer of your dressing table.
   在您的梳妆台中间的抽屉里有客房服务的菜单。

2. Choose the items you like, mark down the time you need it and then hang it outside the doorknob.
   选择您想吃的，标记好您的吃饭时间，然后把它挂在外面的门把手上。

3. You need to hang it before 2: 30 p.m. this afternoon or you may take the chosen menu to the room attendant.
   您需要在下午两点半之前挂在门把手上，或是您可以直接把点好的门把手菜单交给客房服务员。

4. We will offer you breakfast and dinner in your room.
   我们将在您的房间为您提供早餐或晚餐。

5. There is 15% extra charge for room service.
   客房服务加收百分之十五的服务费。

6. There is an extra service charge of 15% for room service.

客房服务加收百分之十五的服务费。

7. For room service, please dial 9, then you will contact with the room attendant and order what you want.

您要想客房订餐,请直接拨打9与客房服务员联系,点您想吃的。

8. For room service, breakfast is served from 7: 30 a.m. to 10: 00 a.m. and the lunch and dinner are served from 11: 30 a.m. to 11: 30 p.m.

客房服务的早餐供应时间为早七点半到早十点。午餐和晚餐的供应时间为早十一点半到晚十一点半。

9. Room service is available 24 hours a day.

客房服务全天候供应。

10. If you want to have your meals in your room, just dial room service.

如果您想在房间里用餐,请直接给客房服务部打电话。

11. You may dial 7, then ask for room service.

如果您想要使用客房服务,请直接拨打7。

12. Would you like to order by phone or by doorknob menu?

您是想通过电话预订还是门把手菜单预订?

语言使用

英文中的数字表达法(二)

1. 英文中时间的读法。

(1)直接法:按照时间顺序直接读出英文。

上午八点钟　读作:eight o'clock in the morning

上午九点零八　读作:nine O eight in the morning

下午二点十五分　读作:two fifteen in the afternoon

晚上七点三十分　读作:seven thirty in the evening

注意:也可直接在时间后面加上"a.m."表示上午,后面加上"p.m."表示下午和晚上。

上午八点钟　读作:eight a.m.

上午九点零八　读作:nine O eight a.m.

下午二点十五分　读作:two fifteen p.m.

晚上七点三十分　读作:seven thirty p.m.

(2)间接法:用past, to 表示时间。第一分钟到第二十九分钟用past;第三十一到第五十九分钟用to,表示差几分钟到下一个整点;第三十分钟用half past;整点同直接法。

上午十点零五分　读作:five (minutes) past ten in the morning

上午七点三十分　读作:half past seven in the morning

下午一点四十　读作:twenty to two in the afternoon

晚上九点五十　读作:ten to ten in the evening

注意：当遇到十五分钟时，可以用 a quarter 表示。

上午十点十五　　读作：a quarter past ten in the morning

下午三点四十五　读作：a quarter to four in the afternoon

2. 英文中分数、小数、百分比的读法。

（1）分数读法：分子用基数词，分母用序数词，分子超过 1，分母加 s。

二分之一　　读作：one second (a half)

三分之一　　读作：one third (a third)

三分之二　　读作：two thirds

（2）小数读法：小数点读作 point，如果小数点后是两位以上的数，则需分别读出每一位。

0.5　　读作：zero point five

0.125　　读作：zero point one two five

（3）百分比读法：百分比只需在数字后加上 percent。

百分之二十五　　读作：twenty five percent

百分之十一点五　　读作：eleven point five percent

3. 电话号码、温度和门牌号的读法。

（1）电话号码读法：每个数字一一读出，遇到零，可读 zero，也可读 O；遇到两个连续一样的数字，可以直接连续读两遍，也可以读 double+ 数字。

306-4322　　读作：three O six four three double two

也可读作：three zero six four three two two

（2）温度：温度分为华氏温度 Fahrenheit 和摄氏温度 Centigrade 两种。

15 ℃　　读作：fifteen degrees centigrade

32 °F　　读作：thirty-two degrees Fahrenheit

（3）门牌号：三位数字，直接读；四位数字，分两个部分读。

Room 309　　读作：Room three zero nine 也可读作：Room three O nine

Room 1520　　读作：Room fifteen twenty

能力训练

情境 1：

两人一组编排对话：Hanks 先生给 room service 打电话，明早八点左右要在房间吃早餐，他点了美式早餐（食物可以自选）。

要求：两人一组，完成对话，注意服务礼仪。

情境 2：

Room service 接到 Miller 女士的电话，她要在房间里吃早餐，她的早餐要清淡一些，因为正在节食，服务员听懂了 Miller 女士的要求并推荐了一些清淡早餐，Miller 女士感到很满意。

要求：两人一组，完成对话，注意服务礼仪。

项目 2　The Housekeeping（客房部）

学习任务 5　Delivering Room Service（客房送餐服务）

工作任务	Delivering Room Service（客房送餐服务）	教学模式	线上线下混合教学模式 情境模拟教学模式
建议学时	2 学时	教学地点	智慧教室或多媒体教室
任务描述	客房服务员早上 7 点 50 分推着餐车来到 Hanks 先生的门外准备为他送餐		
学习目标	1. 掌握中式和西式早餐菜品的英文表达。 2. 掌握客房送餐的服务程序及各个程序里常用的英文语句。 3. 能听懂客人关于客房送餐的投诉。 4. 能用英语向客人解释原因和致歉。 5. 通过学习任务，培养学生有效沟通的能力和优秀的职业素养		

头脑风暴

1．酒店提供的早餐和正餐通常都有什么样的餐品？
2．如果你是客房服务员，你认为客房送餐的服务程序有几个，各个程序应如何与客人进行英语沟通。
3．为客人客房送餐，早餐和正餐的服务程序是否一样？
4．如何处理关于客房送餐的客人投诉？

词汇储备

1. trolley　推车
2. tray　托盘
3. hallway　走廊，过道
4. steak　牛排
5. wine and glass　红酒和杯子
6. fruit salad　水果沙拉
7. pasta　意大利面
8. tuna　金枪鱼
9. salmon　三文鱼
10. sardine　沙丁鱼
11. shrimp　虾
12. lobster　龙虾

13. crab 螃蟹
14. squid 鱿鱼
15. yoghurt 酸奶
16. garden salad 田园沙拉
17. snack basket 小食拼盘
18. fried rice noodles 炒米粉
19. ketchup 番茄酱
20. grilled sausage 烤香肠
21. mustard 芥末
22. sandwich 三明治

服务流程

客房送餐服务流程（电话与当面）如下：

1. Greetings.
   问候。

2. Serving the food.
   为客人提供服务。

   a. Where should the attendant put the food.
      询问客人菜品摆放位置。

   b. Repeating the dishes.
      重复客人所点菜肴。

   c. Asking for permission and giving some reminds to the guest.
      提醒客人注意事项。

3. Asking the guest to sign the name and room number on the bill.
   告知客人签写账单。

4. Expressing the wishes.
   表达祝愿。

客房送餐服务

情境模拟

客房送餐服务流程及句子表达如下：

1. The first step: Greetings.
   第一步：问候。常用的句子有：

   a. Good morning. Room service, may I come in?
      早上好，客房服务，我能进来吗？

   b. Good evening. May I come through?
      晚上好，我能进来吗？

   c. Good morning. Room service, I've brought you the breakfast. May I come in?

早上好，客房服务，我来给您送早餐，我能进来吗？

d. Good evening, I'm here to bring your dinner you have ordered.
   晚上好，我来给您送餐。

情境 1： 上午 8 点，送餐部服务员敲门，准备为 Smith 先生进入房间送餐。
   Good morning, room service, may I come in?

情境 2： 下午，送餐部服务员来到客人房门前，准备敲门进入，为客人送餐。
   Good afternoon, I'm here to bring your dinner you have ordered, may I come in?

2. The second step: Serving the food.
   第二步：为客人提供服务。
   Where should the attendant put the food.
   询问客人菜品摆放位置，常用的句子有：

   a. Where would you like me to put them?
      您想让我把菜放在哪？

   b. Excuse me, may I put your breakfast on the table?
      抱歉打扰您，我能把您的早餐放到桌子上吗？

   c. Where should I put the tray?
      我把托盘放在哪？

   d. Where would you like me to place them?
      我把菜品放在哪里？

      Repeating the dishes.
   重复客人所点菜肴，常用的句子有：

   a. This is your breakfast, we have...
      这是您点的……

   b. Here is your Chinese breakfast... your continental breakfast...
      这是您的中式早餐……您的欧式早餐……

   c. Here is your dinner. Your appetizer...
      这是您点的晚餐，您的开胃菜……

   Some reminders to the guest.
   提醒客人注意事项，常用的句子有：

   a. Shall I serve your meal now, sir?
      先生，您想现在就用餐吗？

   b. Shall I serve the food now or leave it in the hot cupboard?
      我是现在为您上菜还是把菜放到保温盘里？

   c. Shall I open the wine/ beer/ juice, sir?
      先生，我现在能为您把葡萄酒 / 啤酒 / 果汁打开吗？

73

d. Madam, it is a little hot, please be careful!
女士，这道菜有点烫，请当心！

情境 1： 服务员询问客人把早餐放在哪。
Sir, I've brought you your breakfast, where should I put them?

情境 2： 客人点了两份中式早餐、两杯咖啡和两个煎蛋，放好后与客人确认。
Madam, here is your two Chinese breakfast, your coffee and your fried eggs, sunny side down.

情境 3： 与客人确认所点菜肴是否正确。
Sir, this is your appetizer, your medium steak, two pizzas, a fruit salad and a tuna sandwich, is that right?

情境 4： 客人此时不想立刻进餐，给客人一些建议。
Madam, shall I leave the food in the hot cupboard or it will be cold?

3. The third step: Asking the guest to sign the name and room number on the bill.
   第三步：告知客人签写账单。常用的句子有：

   a. Here is your bill, please check it.
      这是您的账单，请您核对一下。

   b. Would you like to sign the bill please, sir?
      先生，您能签一下账单吗？

   c. Would you please sign your name and room number here?
      您能签上您的名字和房间号吗？

   d. Would you please sign your name and room number on the bill?
      您能在账单上签上您的名字和房间号吗？

   e. Would you mind signing your name here?
      您介意在此签名吗？

   f. Would you please sign the bill?
      您能在账单上签上您的名字吗？

   g. We will add your cost to your room bill.
      我们会把费用挂到您的房账上。

   h. We will charge it to your room bill.
      我们会把费用挂到您的房账上。

情境 1： 把账单递给客人，告知客人签名。
Sir, this is your bill, please check it.

情境 2： 客房服务员和客人交流付账事宜。
G: How can I pay the bill?

R: Sir, you may sign the bill or pay in cash. If you would like to sign the bill, we will charge it to your room.

4. The fourth step: Expressing the wishes.
第四步：表达祝愿。常用的句子有：

   a. Thank you for using room service. Enjoy yourself！
      感谢您使用客房送餐，祝您用餐愉快！
   b. Just call me if you need any help. Enjoy your meal, sir.
      先生如果您有什么需要，请联系我们，祝您用餐愉快！
   c. You may leave the trolley in the hallway after you finish your breakfast.
      您用完餐后，可以把手推车放到过道里。
   d. I'll come to collect the dishes when you finish it.
      您用完餐后，我回来给您收拾。
   e. Would you mind ringing the room service when you finish your meal, and we will take the trolley away?
      您用餐完毕后能给 room service 打个电话吗？我们好把餐车给您推走。
   f. If you like, you can leave the trolley outside your door.
      如果您喜欢，您可以把餐车放到门口。

情境 1：祝客人用餐愉快，并告知客人用餐完毕后餐车的摆放位置。
Sir, you may leave the trolley in the hallway after you finish your breakfast. Enjoy yourself. Goodbye.

情境 2：感谢客人使用 room service。
Sir, thank you for using room service. Just call me if you need any help. Enjoy your meal, sir.

能力进阶

酒店客人给客房送餐吧打来电话询问：

Why the breakfast hasn't been sent up yet. He hung his breakfast doorknob menu at 9:00 p.m. before he went to bed the previous night.

1. Answer the call.
   接听电话。
2. Apologize.
   表示抱歉。
3. Promise to send him breakfast right away.
   承诺立刻为客人送餐。

常用表达：

a. I am sorry to hear that.
真的很抱歉。

b. We do apologize for being late for your breakfast.
很抱歉您的早餐送晚了。

c. I am really sorry. We will send your breakfast immediately.
真心抱歉，马上为您送早餐。

d. I am sorry, sir. Your meal will be sent right away. Sorry for the inconvenience.
很抱歉，先生。马上给您送。给您带来不便，请谅解。

对话示例

R: Good morning, Mr. Smith. How may I help you?

G: Good morning. I ordered breakfast for 7 a.m., but it hasn't arrived yet.

R: I am sorry to hear that, Mr. Smith. How did you order, by phone or by doorknob menu?

G: By doorknob menu.

R: When did you hang the menu outside your door?

G: Well, I guess it was around 1 a.m.

R: Oh, I see. The menu should be hung on the doorknob before 12 midnight because we don't collect doorknob menus after midnight. Sorry.

G: I see...but now can you send up something in ten minutes? I am in a hurry.

R: What would you like to have, sir?

G: Some toast and a black coffee.

R: No problem, Mr.Smith. It will be brought up right away.

语言使用

如何用英文表达请求

1. Would you mind +doing 您介意……吗？
   Would you mind moving a little?
   Would you mind signing your name here?

2. Would you please +do 您能……吗？
   Would you please do me a favor?
   Would you please let me know your name?

3. Would you like +n. 您想要……吗？
   Would you like a cup of tea?
   Would you like some some fired noodles?

4. Would you like +to do 您想……吗？
   Would you like to call us when you finish your meal?
   Would you like to drink some fresh juice?

5. Could I +do 我能……吗？
   Could I talk to Mr. Hanks?
   Could I use this pen?

能力训练

情境 1：
游览之后，Miller 小姐感觉十分不舒服，Tina 给她点了客房送餐服务。不久，客房送餐服务员把食物送进客房并询问客人还需要什么帮助。
要求：两人一组，完成对话，注意服务礼仪。

情境 2：
服务员来到 Hanks 先生的房间提供送餐服务，Hanks 先生点了正餐，准备和助手们在房间用餐。为客人提供正餐服务时，要和客人进行交流，要询问客人是否需要马上把酒打开，是否现在需要用餐，是否需要服务，然后告知客人用完餐后把餐车放在门口或给客服中心打电话。
要求：两人一组，完成对话，注意服务礼仪。

能力拓展

客房服务英语 200 句

1. Housekeeping. May I come in?
   我是客房服务员，可以进来吗？
2. When would you like me to do your room, sir?
   您要我什么时间来给您打扫房间呢，先生？
3. You can do it now if you like.
   如果您愿意，现在就可以打扫。
4. I would like you to go and get me a flask of hot water.
   我想请你给我拿一瓶开水来。
5. I'm sorry that your flask is empty.
   很抱歉您的水壶空了。
6. May I do the turn-down service for you now?
   现在可以为您收拾房间了吗？
7. Oh, thank you. But you see, we are having some friends over.
   噢，谢谢，但你知道我们邀请了一些朋友过来聚聚。
8. Could you come back in three hours?
   你能不能过 3 小时再来整理？
9. Certainly, madam. I'll let the overnight staff know.
   当然可以，女士。我会转告夜班服务员。
10. Would you tidy up a bit in the bathroom?

请整理一下浴室好吗？

11. I've just taken a bath and it is quite a mess now.
    我刚洗了澡，那儿乱糟糟的。

12. Besides, please bring us a bottle of just boiled water.
    此外，请给我们带瓶刚烧开的水来。

13. It's growing dark. Would you like me to draw the curtains for you?
    天黑下来了，要不要我拉上窗帘？

14. Is there anything I can do for you?
    您还有什么事要我做吗？

15. I'm always at your service.
    乐意效劳。

16. But before you start, would you do this for me?
    但是在您开始之前，可以帮我做这个吗？

17. Could you come back in three hours?
    您能在3小时后回来吗？

18. Could you send someone up for my laundry?
    请叫人到我的房间收取要洗的衣服，好吗？

19. Certainly, our room attendant will collect in a minute.
    好的，我们的服务员马上就到。

20. Is there anything else I can do for you?
    还有其他我能帮助你的吗？

21. Housekeeping, may I help you?
    这里是客房部，有什么为您效劳吗？

22. I come to collect the laundry.
    我是来收衣的。

23. Excuse me, your clothes are ready.
    打扰一下，您的衣服洗好了。

24. I will take it back and clean it again.
    我会把它带回重新清洁。

25. I'll send someone to your room to check immediately.
    我马上叫人到您的房间检查。

26. Good morning, sir, may I make up the room now?
    早上好，现在可以打扫房间吗？

27. Now is no need, could you like me to come back?
    不，现在不必，我过一会再来好吗？

28. Sure, what time would you like me to come back to clean?
    当然可以，您希望什么时候来打扫？

29. You may make up the room when I go out.
    我出去后再打扫。
30. That is fine.
    好的。
31. Good evening, can I help you?
    晚上好，我能帮助您吗？
32. Turn-down service, may I come in, please?
    开夜床服务，我可以进来吗？
33. Good evening, may I do the turn-down service for you now please?
    晚上好，请问现在可以替您开夜床吗？
34. Not now, could you come in later, please?
    现在不行，你一会过来好吗？
35. Certainly, come in, please.
    可以，进来吧。
36. Thank you, no need more time.
    谢谢，一会儿就好。
37. Is there anything else I can do for you?
    您还需要其他帮助吗？
38. No, thank you.
    没有了，谢谢。
39. You're welcome. It is our pleasure to service our guests.
    不用谢，为客人服务我们感到很荣幸。
40. Certainly, I will get them away now.
    当然可以，我马上就去拿。
41. I will check with my supervisor.
    我要请示一下主管。
42. Have a good time.
    祝您旅途愉快。
43. You arc so helpful. Thank you!
    您真是帮助很大。感谢您！
44. Let me show you the way.
    让我给您指路。
45. This way please.
    请这边走。
46. Sorry, we don't have this kind of the service.
    对不起，我们没有这种服务。
47. I'll send a room attendant up right away.

我马上就让服务员过去。

48. Is that all right?
    这样可以吗？

49. No hot water.
    没有热水。

50. The toilet is stopped up.
    马桶堵塞。

51. Yes, go ahead.
    是的，可以的。

52. Leave your laundry in the laundry in the laundry bag behind the bathroom door.
    请把要洗的东西放在浴室门后的洗衣袋中。

53. I hope I'm not disturbing you.
    我希望没有打扰您。

54. What is your room number?
    您的房间号码是多少？

55. Sure./ Certainly.
    当然可以。

56. One moment, madam. I'll bring them to you right away.
    等一会儿，夫人。我马上送来。

57. I'll send for an electrician (doctor...).
    我给您请电工（大夫……）。

58. I'll be there in a few minutes.
    我马上就去。

59. This is a check-out room.
    此为走房。

60. The lines to be repaired and washed.
    需要修补和清洗的部件。

61. We'll send some houseman to your room.
    我们会派房间男工来您房间。

62. I'll send a plumber to your room.
    我们会派一个水管工来您房间。

63. I'm the housekeeper, may I help you?
    我是客房主任，需要帮助吗？

64. You can put the DND sign outside your door.
    您可以在您的房间外悬挂"请勿打扰"牌。

65. We're responsible for the baby-sitting service too.
    我们也负责托婴服务。

66. The turn-down service is necessary for you, sir.
    先生，晚床服务是很有必要的。

67. The tears and wears in the guest room.
    客房内的物品用旧及损坏。

68. My room is a mess.
    我的房间一团乱。

69. It's so noisy right outside my door, and I can't sleep.
    房门外太吵了，我无法入睡。

70. Please contact the front office.
    请联系前台。

71. Don't hesitate to contact us if you have anything emergent.
    如遇紧急事件，请随时联系我们。

72. For turn-down service, I'll switch on certain lights.
    对于晚床服务，我会打开一些灯。

73. Shall I pay for the damage I made in my room?
    我应该赔偿我造成的房间内损坏吗？

74. I'm afraid you have to sir.
    先生，恐怕您必须这样做。

75. One more thing, the minibar needs refilling.
    还有件事情，迷你吧需要重新装填。

76. The towels are dirty.
    毛巾脏了。

77. Please empty the waste bin.
    请倾倒垃圾筒。

78. The shampoo in my restroom is spilt.
    我洗手间内的洗发液洒了。

79. The sink needs wiping, I'm afraid.
    恐怕洗水槽需要被清洁。

80. By the way, I broke the vase by accident.
    顺便说下，我无意打破了花盆。

81. I've run into something urgent about my room.
    关于我的房间我遇到了一些紧急事件。

82. I was about to take a shower in the restroom.
    我当时刚要在洗手间洗澡。

83. No hot water for shower was available.
    没有淋浴用的热水。

84. These shower controls are difficult to use.

这些淋浴设备控制开关很难使用。

85. The room attendant showed the gentleman how to use the shower controls.
    房间服务员教这位先生如何使用淋浴控制开关。

86. This is Mr.Giant calling from Room 3008.
    我是3008房间的基恩特先生。

87. There seems to be something wrong with the toilet.
    马桶好像出问题了。

88. The toilet doesn't flush.
    马桶不冲水。

89. What seems to be the trouble?
    哪里出问题了？

90. The bath room looks like a huge mess now.
    洗手间现在一团糟。

91. I'm sorry to hear that, but don't worry.
    听到这个消息我很难过，但别担心。

92. I'll try to fix it immediately.
    我会立刻处理此事。

93. How to deal with the damage caused by the guest.
    如何处理客人造成的损坏。

94. I'll vacuum the carpet in your room.
    我来用吸尘器打扫你房间内的地毯。

95. We'll send someone to collect your laundries.
    我们会派专人收集您要洗的衣物。

96. Please leave the laundries in your laundry bag.
    请将要洗衣物放置在洗衣袋内。

97. Don't forget to fill in the laundry list by the way.
    别忘记顺便填上洗衣清单。

98. Please draw the curtains close.
    请拉上窗帘。

99. We are not allowed to do that.
    我们不允许那样做。

100. We are not allowed to answer phone calls for the guest when the guest is not in.
     当客人外出的时候，我们不允许接听客房内的电话。

101. This is the room regulation of our hotel.
     这是酒店内的关于客房的规定。

102. Sometimes we will look after guest's child on request.
     有时候我们会根据客人的要求照顾客人的孩子。

103. Providing such things on request as blanket, extra bed, etc.
 根据要求提供毛毯、加床等。

104. You can hang the DND sign if you don't want to be disturbed.
 如果不想被打扰，请悬挂免扰牌。

105. Shall I get you a doctor?
 我能为您叫医生吗？

106. I hope you feel better soon.
 我希望您会尽快好起来。

107. We can't offer you any medicine, I'm afraid.
 恐怕我们不可以为您提供药物。

108. I'll know you want us to clean your room then.
 我知道您想我们清理您的房间。

109. The TV set is not running correctly.
 电视机有问题。

110. The minijar doesn't work.
 热水器不工作。

111. This is our hotel's prime duty to serve.
 这是我们酒店服务的最大职责。

112. I'll keep a note of that.
 我会记住的。

113. In case there's something urgent.
 以防有紧急事件发生。

114. Guests' request for extra things.
 客人要求额外物品。

115. The guest in room 4008 need an extra pillow.
 4008房间的客人需要一个额外的枕头。

116. I'm afraid it's charged.
 恐怕这是收费的。

117. The hair drier has to be under your request, madam.
 夫人，吹风机只能在您要求时候提供。

118. I'll contact the staff in charge.
 我会联系负责人的。

119. I'm not allowed to take any tip, but thank you all the same.
 我不允许收取小费，但是还是感谢您。

120. Put the documents in good order.
 把文件摆放好。

121. Your room is in perfect condition for your stay.

对于您的入住，房间已经准备妥当。

122. I appreciate your help with the room condition.
    对于房间内的状况，我感谢你的帮助。

123. The former guest in this room left some personal things.
    前任房间客人遗留下一些私人物品。

124. The room is tidy and ready now.
    房间准备妥当。

125. Sorry to have kept you waiting.
    抱歉让您久等。

126. There is no lamp-shade in my room.
    我的房间内没有台灯灯罩。

127. Do you provide personal services like shoe-polishing?
    你们提供像擦鞋这样的私人服务吗？

128. The curtain is torn.
    窗帘已坏。

129. Do you offer wake-up call for me?
    你们给我提供唤醒服务吗？

130. The ashtray is broken partly.
    烟灰缸有一部分坏了。

131. But I didn't break the cup.
    但是我没有打坏杯子。

132. The pillow case is very dirty.
    枕头套很脏。

133. She talked to a floor attendant.
    她对一楼层服务员交谈。

134. Someone knocked the door of the guest room.
    有人敲客房的门。

135. May I have a local newspaper to read?
    我可以要份当地报纸阅读吗？

136. Can I take away the newspaper to my room?
    我可以将报纸带回房间内吗？

137. You can only read it here I'm afraid.
    恐怕您只能在此阅读。

138. Can you call a taxi for me please?
    您可以为我叫辆出租车吗？

139. This is my first time staying in your hotel.
    这是我第一次在贵酒店入住。

140. I'm afraid I can't leave my post.
 恐怕我不能离岗。

141. I'll call the concierge for you if you like.
 如果您需要，我可以为您召唤礼宾员。

142. I'll contact the babysitter for you right now.
 我立刻为您联系托婴员。

143. Would you mind sending someone to my room now?
 您可以现在派人前往我房间吗？

144. The babysitter is so responsible.
 托婴员如此负责。

145. We are trained to be responsible.
 我们受过负责任的训练。

146. How much should I pay for the baby-sitting service?
 托婴服务怎么收费的？

147. Are there any formalities I have to follow through?
 我应该办理一些手续吗？

148. How can I pay for the extra room service?
 额外的房间送餐服务怎么付款？

149. This is the room center.
 这里是客房中心。

150. Our staff are all reliable and experienced.
 我们的员工都很可靠，经验丰富。

151. I have some clothes to be washed.
 我需要清洗一些衣物。

152. Just leave it in the laundry bag in your wardrobe.
 把它放在您的大衣柜内洗衣袋里就可以了。

153. Otherwise the hotel count will be accepted as correct.
 否则，酒店计数将被视为正确。

154. What's the difference in price?
 价格有何差别？

155. We provide the normal service and express service.
 我们提供普通服务和加急服务。

156. We charge 30% more for the service.
 对于此项服务我们加收 30% 的费用。

157. How long does it usually take to have laundry done?
 洗好衣服经常花多久时间？

158. A button came off my coat.

我的大衣上一个纽扣脱落了。

159. Can you sew on a new one for me?
     您能为我缝补上一枚新的吗?

160. What if there is any laundry damage?
     如果有衣物损坏怎么办?

161. In such a case, the hotel will certainly pay for it.
     这样的话,酒店一定会赔偿的。

162. The indemnity should not exceed ten times of the laundry charge.
     赔偿金额不能超过洗衣费用的 10 倍。

163. A guest steps in the housekeeper's room angrily.
     一位客人生气地走进客房经理的房间。

164. I was just in my room and the door was locked.
     我当时在房内,而且房门已上锁。

165. It can only be one of your staff.
     只可能是你们其中一位员工做的。

166. Well, I can very well understand you are upset about it.
     嗯,我完全能够理解您对此事感到不安。

167. We will do our best to help you about your room condition.
     我们会尽全力帮助您了解您房间状况。

168. But first, I will have one of my staff look through your room.
     但是首先我会派员工检查您的房间。

169. I must say we can not be held responsible.
     我必须说我们不承担责任。

170. You may deposit your valuables in the safe-deposit box.
     您可以将贵重物品寄存在保险柜里。

171. Our receptionist must have given you such advice when you checked in.
     我们接待人员一定已经在您登记入住时给了您这样的建议。

172. It says so on your key card.
     您的房卡上也有注明。

173. When can the guest get his laundry back?
     客人何时能取回洗好的衣服?

174. The hotel's policy on the laundry damage is clear.
     酒店关于洗衣服务的规定是很明白的。

175. Would you please send a doctor form your clinic for me?
     您可以为我从医疗室派一位医生过来吗?

176. My husband has slipped in the bathroom, he can't stand.
     我的丈夫在洗手间滑倒了,无法站立。

177. Can you bring two more chairs to my room? I have some visitors later.
我一会有些客人到来，您能送来我房间一些额外的椅子吗？

178. I'll bring a towel for you to clean it.
我会给您送来一条毛巾清理用。

179. Could you offer me an extra bed for our little child?
您能够给我们的小孩子提供一张额外的床吗？

180. I know it's not free of charge.
我知道这不是免费的。

181. High quality service is the most important product.
高质量的服务是最重要的产品。

182. She works as a room attendant recently.
她最近做客房服务员。

183. Problems on the night shift for the room attendant.
客房服务员的夜班问题。

184. They have some negative comments on our management work of guest rooms.
他们对我们客房管理工作有些消极的评论。

185. We'll do what we can to improve our service.
我们会尽全力改善我们的服务。

186. My stay in this room has been pleasant.
我在这个房间过得很愉快。

187. What's the best time to do the repair in the guest room?
客房打扫服务何时最佳？

188. You need to comfort the guest.
你需要安慰客人。

189. You promise to have someone to have it checked.
你答应过派专人进行核查。

190. The room condition is really disappointing.
客房状况真的让人失望。

191. The visitor's stay can't exceed two hours.
访客的逗留不可以超过2个小时。

192. The light bulb of my bed side lamp isn't working.
我床头边台灯灯泡不亮了。

193. May I make long distance calls directly in my room?
我房间内可以直拨长途电话吗？

194. The local calls need to be operated by our operator.
本地电话需要我们接线员转接。

195. The heating system in my room seems refuse to work.

我房间内供热系统不管用了。

196. I'll demonstrate how to use it in your restroom.
我会教您如何在您房间内使用它的。

197. I'm afraid this is one–off item in the bedroom.
恐怕这是您房间内一次性用品。

198. Let me have a check on your curtain.
让我检查下您的窗帘。

199. How to use the key card to open my door?
怎样使用房卡开房门啊？

200. What if I lose my key card? Shall I pay for it?
如果房卡丢失怎么办？我应该赔偿吗？

项目 3

The Food & Beverage（餐饮部）

学习任务 1　Booking a Table（预订餐台服务）

工作任务	Booking a Table （预订餐台服务）	教学模式	线上线下混合教学模式 情境模拟教学模式
建议学时	4 学时	教学地点	智慧教室或多媒体教室
任务描述	某天上午，住店客人 Hanks 先生打电话到餐厅，想预订玫瑰餐厅大厅的非吸烟的一张两人餐台，他的用餐时间大概是晚上 7 点		
学习目标	1. 掌握餐桌预订的相关词汇。 2. 掌握电话订餐的工作服务流程。 3. 熟练地用英文受理电话和当面预订餐台服务。 4. 熟知电话用语应有的礼仪和禁忌。 5. 掌握"我想要……"和"我能……吗？"的委婉表达。 6. 培养学生不怕吃苦、精益求精等优秀品质		

酒店服务英语

头脑风暴

1. 你以前有过类似的经历吗？相关英语表达你会吗？如"靠窗的桌子""两人台"等。
2. 如果你是酒店餐厅服务员，给客人电话预订餐台或当面受理客人预订的时候，你会询问客人哪些问题呢？
3. 如果预订已满，怎么用英语与客人沟通？

词汇储备

1. reservation *n.* 预订 reserve *v.* 预订 reserve=book
2. table reservation 餐桌预订
3. reservationist 预订员
4. waiter/waitress 餐厅服务员
5. host/hostess 引位员
6. private room 包房
7. peak season/peak time/peak hour 高峰期
8. non-smoking area 非吸烟区
9. a table in the lobby/hall 大厅餐台
10. a table by the south 靠南边的桌子
11. a table by the window 靠窗的桌子
12. a table near/next to the window 靠窗的桌子
13. arrange *v.* 安排 arrangement *n.* 安排
14. minimum charge 最低消费
15. buffet *n.* 自助餐
16. exclude *v.* 不包括 include *v.* 包括
17. guarantee *v.* 确保；保证

服务流程

餐桌预订服务流程如下：

1. Greetings.
   问候。
2. Asking the guest the reservation information.
   询问客人预订信息。
   （1）arrival date and time.
       到达日期和时间。
   （2）number of guests.
       客人数量。

预订包房服务

预订餐位服务

（3）special requests.

特殊需求。

3. Asking the guest the personal information.

询问客人个人信息。

4. Confirming reservation.

确认信息。

5. Expressing the wishes.

表达祝愿。

情境模拟

1. The first step: Greetings.

第一步：问候。常用的句子有：

a. Good afternoon, Welcome to Hilton Hotel. May I help you?

下午好，希尔顿酒店，有什么能帮到您的？

b. Good morning, Garden Restaurant. What can I do for you?

早上好，花园餐厅，您有什么需要吗？

c. Good afternoon, Spring Restaurant. How may I help you?

晚上好，春天餐厅，有什么能帮到您的？

d. Good afternoon, Mr. Hanks. May I help you?

下午好，Hanks 先生。有什么能帮到您的？

情境 1： 上午 10 点，一位女士和一位先生来到春天餐厅，想要预订一个餐位。

Good morning, sir and madam. Welcome to Spring Restaurant. What can I do for you?

情境 2： 住店客人 Smith 先生下午 4 点来到花园餐厅，想要预订一个餐位。

Good afternoon, Mr. Smith. May I help you?

情境 3： 一位女士通过打电话的方式，想要预订一个餐位。

Good evening, Garden Restaurant. How may I help you?

2. The second step: Asking the guest the reservation information.

第二步：询问客人预订需求。

（1）arrival date and time.

到达日期和时间。

（2）number of guests.

客人数量。

（3）special requests.

特殊需求。

询问到达日期和时间，常用的句子有：

a. When would you like your table?
   您（你们）哪天来呢？
b. For which date?
   请问是哪天？
c. What time will you be arriving?
   您（你们）几点能到？
d. (At) what time should we expect you?
   您（你们）几点能到？

询问客人一行有多少人，常用的句子有：

a. For how many people/persons?
   一共多少人？
b. How many people/persons are there in your party?
   一行共多少人？

询问特殊需求，常用的句子有：

a. Do you have any special requests?
   您有什么特殊需求吗？
b. Any special requests, sir?
   先生，您有什么特殊需求吗？

情境 1：住店客人 Smith 先生来到餐厅订餐，询问其用餐日期和用餐时间。
Mr. Smith, for which date and what time will you be arriving?

情境 2：一位女士电话订餐，询问其用餐人数。
How many persons are there in your party, madam?

情境 3：客人电话订餐，询问其有无特殊需求。
Sir/Madam, do you have any special requests?

3. The third step: Asking the guest the personal information.

第三步：询问客人个人信息。常用的句子有：

a. May I have your name and telephone number?
   能告诉我您的名字和电话吗？
b. May I know your name and contact number?
   我可以知道您的名字和联系电话吗？
c. May I know your room number?
   我可以知道您的房间号吗？

情境 1：如何询问住店客人 Smith 先生的联系方式和房间号。
Mr. Smith, may I know your room number, please?

情境 2：电话询问男性客人的个人信息。

　　May I have your name and telephone number, sir?

4. The fourth step: Confirming reservation.

第四步：确认预订信息。常用的句子有：

a. Sir, I'd like to confirm your reservation...Am I right?
   先生，我确认一下您的预订信息……对吗？
b. Let me confirm your reservation...Is that correct?
   我确认一下您的预订信息……对吗？
c. So, Mr.Smith, you have booked...Is that right?
   Smith 先生，您预订了……对吗？

情境 1：住店客人 Smith 先生预订了一张今晚 6 点的两人台，和 Smith 先生当面确认一下预订信息。

　　So, Mr.Smith, you have booked a table for two at 6 o'clock this evening. Is that right?

情境 2：一位女士电话预订了本周六晚 7 点的一张八人台，与客人确认预订信息。

　　Madam, I'd like to confirm your reservation, you booked a table for eight at 7 o'clock this Saturday. Am I right?

情境 3：一位男士电话预订明晚 5 点的两张两人台，要求都在二楼靠窗的非吸烟区，与客人确认预订信息。

　　Sir, let me confirm your reservation, you reserved two tables for two by the window in the non-smoking area on the second floor. Is that correct?

5. The fifth step: Expressing the wishes.

第五步：表达祝愿。常用的句子有：

a. We look forward to serving you.
   期待着为您服务。
b. We look forward to seeing you tonight.
   期待着今晚见到您。
c. We look forward to your arrival.
   期待着您的光临。
d. Thank you for your reserving. Hope to see you soon.
   感谢您的预订，希望尽快见到您。

情境 1：住店客人 Hanks 先生预订完，与 Hanks 先生道别。

　　Mr. Hanks, we look forward to serving you.

情境 2： 一女性客人电话预订完餐位，与客人道别。

Thank you for your reserving. Hope to see you soon, madam.

能力进阶

预订已满（客人打电话到玫瑰餐厅，想要今晚在此就餐，但今晚 8 点前的餐位都已订满）

1. The first step: Greetings.
   第一步：问候。
2. The second step: Asking the guest the reservation information.
   第二步：询问客人预订需求。
   （1）arrival date and time.
      到达日期和时间。
   （2）number of guests.
      客人数量。
   （3）special requests.
      特殊需求。
3. The third step: Telling the guest that the restaurant is fully booked now.
   第三步：告知客人餐厅此时预订已满。
   a. I am sorry, sir. All the private rooms are reserved/booked.
      很抱歉，先生。所有的包房都已经订满了。
   b. I am afraid that the house is full at that time.
      恐怕那个时间餐厅都已订满。
   c. I am sorry that we are fully booked at that time.
      很抱歉，那段时间我们预订已满。
4. The fourth step: Recommending other options for the guest.
   第四步：为客人推荐其他选择。
   （1）changing time.
      更改时间。
   （2）changing table.
      更改餐位。
   （3）waiting for a while if possible.
      如愿意可以等待一会儿再安排。
   a. What about a table in the lobby?
      大厅的餐位怎么样？
   b. May I suggest a private room? It is very quiet.
      包房怎么样？包房的环境非常安静。
   c. Would you please have your table at a later time?

您能延后一小时吗？

5. The fifth step: Confirming reservation.

    第五步：确认预订信息。

6. The sixth step: Expressing the wishes.

    第六步：表达祝愿。

宴会预订 Banquet booking

1. The first step: Greetings.

    第一步：问候。

2. The second step: Asking the details.

    第二步：询问详细信息。常用的句子有：

    （1）expected number of persons   预计到场人数

    a. For how many people?

    b. How many persons?

    有多少人？

    （2）the number of tables needed   多少桌

    a. How many tables would you like?

    b. For how many tables?

    您预订多少桌？

    （3）time of the banquet   宴会时间

    a. When will the event be held?

    b. When would it be?

    c. When would you like your banquet?

    宴会什么时候举行？

    （4）budgets for the banquet   折扣

    a. How much would you like to spend for each table?

    每桌您预算多少？

    b. We always have discount for banquet booking.

    对于宴会预订，我们会给您打折。

    （5）special requests   特殊需求

    a. Do you have any special requests?

    您有什么特殊需求？

    b. Any special requests?

    您有什么特殊需求？

    c. Are there any special requests for the banquet menu?

    对于宴会菜单，您有什么特殊需求？

3. The third step: Asking the personal information.

    第三步：询问联系人信息。

（1）contact name

　　联系人姓名

（2）contact telephone number

　　联系电话

May I have your name and fax number? We may fax you the menu and the wine list for your discussing.

您的名字和传真号是多少？我们会把菜单和酒单发传真给您，供您参考。

4. The fourth step: Asking the guest to pay for the deposit in advance.

   第四步：让客人提前付押金。

   a. How would you like to pay for the deposit?

   　 您打算以什么方式支付押金？

   b. We need the deposit for banquet booking.

   　 对于宴会预订，我们需要您支付押金。

   c. Sir, you need to pay the deposit in advance.

   　 先生，您需要提前支付押金。

5. The fifth step: Confirming.

   第五步：确认。

6. The sixth step: Expressing the wishes.

   第六步：表达祝愿。

语言使用

形容词的用法

1. 形容词是用来描述人或事物的词，可以用于名词之前。

   We offer different drinks.

   Sorry, we don't have any vacant rooms.

   We sell hot and cold drinks.

2. 形容词用于 something, everything, someone, anyone, anything, somewhere 等不定代词之后。

   I would like to have something cold to drink.

   Would you like something new?

3. 形容词用于 be 动词或感官动词（taste, sound, smell, feel, look, seem 等）之后。

   Our manager is very nice.

   The wine tastes perfect.

   That sounds reasonable.

4. 动词 –ing 形式的形容词，用来描述事物对人的影响或人的特点。

   The film was really interesting.

   He was reading a fascinating article.

5. 动词 –ed 形式的形容词，用来描述某人的特点和感受。

We are interested in the new functions of the machine.

She seems excited about the results.

副词的用法

1. 修饰形容词和副词（如 very, quite, awfully）。

   I am awfully sorry for that.

   I am terribly sorry for doing that.

2. 表示发生频率的副词（如 sometimes, always, often, never 等）。

   We always give discount for group reservation.

3. 表示动作的程度（happy–happily, kind–kindly, angry–angrily）。

   They played happily together in their house yesterday.

   He serves very well in his field.

   He can speak 3 foreign languages well.

4. 表示事情发生的可能性。

   We may arrange that for you if it is possibly accepted.

能力训练

情境 1：

上午，住店客人 Hanks 先生打电话到餐厅，想预订一个大厅的两人餐台，在非吸烟区。他的用餐时间大概是晚上 7 点。

要求：每两人一组，一名学生扮演 Hanks 先生，一名学生扮演预订员，服务程序全面。

情境 2：

Smith 先生来到 Hilton 酒店的 Spring Restaurant，想要预订晚上 6 点左右的一张靠窗三人台，被服务员告知晚上 6 点的大厅餐台都已预订满。这时，作为餐厅服务员，该如何处理？

要求：每两人一组，一名学生扮演 Hanks 先生，一名学生扮演预订员，服务程序全面。

学习任务 2　Leading the Guest（引客入位服务）

工作任务	Leading the Guest（引客入位服务）	教学模式	线上线下混合教学模式 情境模拟教学模式
建议学时	4 学时	教学地点	智慧教室或多媒体教室
任务描述	Hanks 先生已经在沈阳丽都索菲特酒店的餐厅做了预订，他与其他几个朋友一起来到餐厅用餐		
学习目标	1. 掌握餐厅领位的服务流程。 2. 掌握工作流程里常用的英文语句。 3. 能够熟练地用英文为有预订的客人领位。 4. 能够熟练地用英文为没有预订的客人领位。 5. 能用英文询问客人有无其他需求，并满足客人需求。 6. 通过训练，培养学生有效沟通的能力。 7. 通过工作流程训练，培养学生严谨敬业的工作作风		

头脑风暴

1. 对于有预订和没有预订的客人，领位时有什么不同要求？
2. 如果你是酒店餐厅服务员，给客人领位时应该注意什么？
3. 针对不同客人需求，你如何应对？

词汇储备

1. Cash Desk=Cashier Counter　收银台
2. cash　现金
3. cashier　收银员
4. currency　货币
5. foreign currency　foreign currencies　外币
6. exchange　交换，兑换
7. exchange rate　兑换率
8. exchange memo　外币兑换水单
9. lobby　大厅
10. private room　雅间（包房）

服务流程

引客入位服务流程如下：
1. Greetings.
   问候。

引客入位
（没有预订）

引客入位
（有预订）

2. Asking the guest if he has a reservation.
   询问客人是否有预订。

3. Asking the guest his dining preference.
   询问客人用餐座位要求。

4. Leading the guests to the table he wants (if necessary).
   引领客人到他满意的餐台就座（如果需要的话）。

5. Expressing the wishes.
   表达祝愿。

情境模拟

1. The first step: Greetings.
   第一步：问候。常用的句子有：
   a. Good morning, sir/ madam. What can I do for you?
   b. Good morning, sir/ madam. May I help you?
   c. Good morning, sir/ madam. Is there anything I can do for you?
   d. Good morning, sir/ madam. How can I help you?
      早上好，先生/女士，请问能为您做什么？

2. The second step: asking the guest if he has a reservation.
   第二步：询问客人是否有预订。常用的句子有：
   a. Do you have a reservation?
   b. Have you made a reservation?
      您有预订吗？

情境 1：住店客人 Hanks 先生来到酒店乐轩华中餐厅（Le Chinois），想在此用午餐。
   Good morning, Mr. Hanks. Have you made a reservation?

情境 2：Smith 先生下午来到酒店丽都西餐厅（Café Lido）用餐。
   Good afternoon, sir. Do you have a reservation?

3. The third step: asking the guest his dining preference.
   第三步：询问客人用餐座位要求。常用的句子有：
   a. How many people are there in your party?
      您一共几位？
   b. Which table would you like?
      您喜欢哪里的餐台？
   c. Would you like to sit in the smoking or non-smoking area?
      您喜欢坐在吸烟区还是非吸烟区？
   d. Where would you like your table, in the lobby or a private room?

您想在哪里用餐，大厅还是包房？

e. Will this table be OK?
这张餐台怎么样？

f. Is this table to your satisfaction?
您对这个餐台满意吗？

g. Do you have any special requests?
您还有其他要求吗？

情境 1： 住店客人 Hanks 先生已经在酒店乐轩华中餐厅（Le Chinois）预订了一个包房。
Mr. Hanks, you've booked a private room at Le Chinois.

情境 2： Smith 先生想在酒店丽都西餐厅（Café Lido）用餐，餐厅服务人员需要询问他对餐台的要求。
How many people are there in your party, sir? Which table would you like, sir? Do you have any special requests?

4. The fourth step: Leading the guests to the table he wants.
   第四步：引领客人到他满意的餐台就座。常用的句子有：

   a. This way, please.
      这边请。

   b. I'll show you to your table.
      我领您去你的座位。

   c. Mind your steps, please.
      请您当心脚下。

情境 1： 住店客人 Hanks 先生预订的包房在四楼，需要坐电梯到达。
Mr. Hanks, the private room is on the 4th floor, we'll take the elevator there. Mind your steps, please.

情境 2： 由于 Smith 先生的餐台在一楼，领位员带他到餐台。
I'll show you to your table, sir, this way, please.

5. The fifth step: Expressing the wishes.
   第五步：表达祝愿。常用的句子有：

   a. (I) hope you'll have a nice meal.
      祝您用餐愉快。

   b. The waiter will take your order later.
      一会儿服务员会为您点餐。

   c. I hope you enjoy your dinner.
      祝您用餐愉快。

项目3　The Food & Beverage（餐饮部）

能力进阶

领位过程中，遇到特殊情况（需要坐电梯）时常用的句子有：

a．We'll take the elevator to your table.
我们坐电梯到您的餐位。

b．Mind your steps please.
当心脚下。

c．The elevator is over there, next to the corridor, after me please.
电梯在那边，挨着走廊，请随我来。

领位过程中，遇到特殊情况（其中一位客人带着小孩）位常用的句子有：

a．Take good care of your kid please.

b．Be careful of your child.
请照看好您的小孩。

语言使用

祈使句

祈使句表达的语气总体来说比较强硬，尤其在表示命令或警告时。当用祈使句表达建议或请求时，可以在句子里加上 please 来缓和语气或表示恳求。

例如：Be quiet, please. 请安静。

Follow me, please. 请跟我来。

Mind your steps, please. 当心脚下。

Have a nice day! 祝您愉快！

能力训练

情境 1：

Hanks 先生和朋友如期来到餐厅用餐，领位员热情地接待了他们，由于雅间在二楼，所以领位员建议走楼梯，并提醒客人当心脚下。

要求：以小组为单位总结出服务员的英文应对语句。

情境 2：

Hanks 先生和朋友如期来到餐厅用餐，领位员热情地接待了他们，看到一位客人带着小孩来就餐，领位员提醒客人注意孩子安全。

要求：以小组为单位总结出服务员的英文应对语句。

101

学习任务3　Serving Chinese Food（中餐服务）

工作任务	Serving Chinese Food（中餐服务）	教学模式	线上线下混合教学模式 情境模拟教学模式
建议学时	6学时	教学地点	智慧教室或多媒体教室
任务描述	Hanks先生等一行七人入住沈阳丽都索菲特酒店后，对酒店提供的接待及商务服务都非常满意，酒店让Hanks等人感受到宾至如归的感觉。接下来，他们要体验中餐服务		
学习目标	1. 掌握中餐点菜的服务程序。 2. 掌握向客人推荐菜肴的方法。 3. 掌握中餐点菜流程里常用的英文表达。 4. 了解中餐菜系及菜名翻译。 5. 能够为客人推荐菜品并做席间服务。 6. 通过训练，培养学生有效沟通的能力。 7. 通过工作流程训练，培养学生具备宾至如归的道德观		

头脑风暴

1. 你了解中国八大菜系吗？
2. 酒店中餐菜品你知道多少？你会用英文表达哪些中餐的菜名？
3. 如何给客人推荐菜肴？

词汇储备

餐厅服务人员 Staff

reservationist　预订员　　　　hostess　迎宾员/领位员　　　director　总监
waiter　服务员　　　　　　　　waitress　女服务员　　　　　manager　经理

形容菜肴

crisp　酥脆的　　　　　　　　tasty　可口的　　　　　　　　tender　鲜嫩的
clear　清淡的　　　　　　　　strong　浓烈的　　　　　　　spicy　麻辣的

蔬菜类 Vegetable

cabbage　白菜　　　　celery　芹菜　　　　turnip　萝卜　　　　carrot　胡萝卜
cucumber　黄瓜　　　　spinach　菠菜　　　onion　洋葱　　　　eggplant　茄子
broccoli　西兰花

烹饪方式 Cooking methods

fry　煎　　　　stir-fry　炒　　　　deep-fry　炸　　　　stew　烩/炖　　　　bake　烘

| smoke 熏 | boil 煮 | roast 烤 | steam 蒸 | braise 红烧 |
| barbecue 烧烤 | simmer 煨/焖 | quick-fry 爆炒 | | |

服务流程

中餐点菜服务流程如下：

1. Greetings and handing the menu.
   问候客人并递上菜单。
2. Ordering and recommending the dishes.
   给客人推荐菜肴并点菜。
3. Confirming the dishes for the guest.
   给客人重复菜单。
4. Expressing the wishes.
   祝客人用餐愉快。

中餐点菜服务

席间服务

情境模拟

1. The first step: Greetings and handing the menu.
   第一步：问候客人并递上菜单。常用的句子有：
   a. Good evening, sir. Here's the menu.
      晚上好，先生，给您菜单。
   b. Good afternoon, ladies and gentlemen. Here are the menu and wine list. You may have a look at it.
      先生们、女士们，下午好。给您菜单和酒单看一看。
   c. Please take your time.
      请您慢慢看。

   情境1：上午11点，住店客人Hanks先生来到酒店乐轩华中餐厅（Le Chinois）预订好的雅间就座，想在此用午餐。
   Good morning, Mr. Hanks. Here's the menu. Please take your time.

   情境2：下午4点30分，进店客人Smith先生在酒店乐轩华中餐厅（Le Chinois）大厅就座。
   Good afternoon, sir. Here's the menu. You may have a look at it.

2. The second step: ordering and recommending the dishes
   第二步：给客人推荐菜肴并点菜。常用的句子有：
   a. Is there anything you can't eat?
      您有什么忌口的吗？
   b. May I suggest the...it's our house specialty.
      我建议您点……，它是我们餐厅招牌菜。

c. Would you like to try...? it's our chef's recommendation.
    试试……怎么样？它是我们的厨师推荐。
d. What about...? It's very popular among the guest.
    ……怎么样？这道菜很受欢迎。
e. I'm afraid it will take some time to prepare.
    这道菜需较长时间准备。
f. It looks good, smells good and tastes good.
    这道菜色香味俱全。

情境 1： 住店客人 Hanks 先生吃中餐的次数不多，餐厅服务员向他推荐本店特色。

Mr. Hanks, would you like to try steamed wild fish head with chopped peppers? it's our chef's recommendation. And you may also try barbecued pork bun, yangmu sheep liver, shrimp balls, and so on.

情境 2： Smith 先生不吃辣，餐厅服务员了解情况并推荐菜品。

Sir, since you would not like to have spicy food, how about old style pot pork? It's our house specialty.

3. The third step: Confirming the dishes for the guest.
   第三步：给客人重复菜单。常用的句子有：
   a. So you'd like to have..., am I correct?
       您点了……，对吗？
   b. So that's ..., anything else, please?
       您点了……，还需要其他的吗？
   c. Where would you like your table, in the lobby or a private room?
       您想在哪里用餐，大厅还是包房？

情境 1： 住店客人 Hanks 先生在中餐厅点了叉烧包、养目羊肝、虾球、老式锅包肉、双色剁椒蒸野生鱼头，餐厅服务员跟客人核对。

Mr. Hanks, you have ordered barbecued pork bun, yangmu sheep liver, shrimp balls and steamed wild fish head with chopped peppers, is that right?

情境 2： 餐厅服务员 Helen 向 Smith 先生重复菜单。

So that's old style pot pork, anything else, sir?

4. The fourth step: Expressing the wishes.
   第四步：祝客人用餐愉快。常用的句子有：
   a. Thank you, sir. Your dishes will be served in a minute.
       谢谢您，先生。您点的菜马上就好。

b. Your order will be ready in a few minutes.

您点的菜马上就好。

c. Have a nice meal.

祝您用餐愉快。

席间服务

a. The dish is very hot, please be careful.

这道菜很热，请当心。

b. Shall I serve the dishes now?

现在可以上菜了吗？

c. Excuse me, sir/ma'am. May I serve the dishes now?

打扰了，先生 / 女士，现在可以上菜了吗？

d. Would you like us to serve the dishes now?

我们现在可以上菜了吗？

e. This is the roasted suckling pig collection. The castor sugar（细砂糖）and chutney（甜面酱）are for it. Please enjoy it.

这是烤乳猪，可以配砂糖和甜面酱，请慢用。

f. Excuse me, sir/ma'am. May I separate the dish for everyone?

打扰了，先生 / 女士。我现在可以给您分鱼了吗？

g. Would you like to separate the fish?

我现在可以给您分鱼了吗？

h. Excuse me, sir/ma'am. May I change the plate for you?

打扰了，先生 / 女士。我现在可以换盘子了吗？

i. May I take the glass away?

我可以把杯子拿走吗？

j. Are you enjoying your meal?

您觉得这些菜怎么样？

k. How do you like the fish?

您想要几分熟的鱼？

注：席间服务包括分菜、换盘和撤盘等。

能力进阶

介绍菜系的常用句子

1. There are eight styles of cuisine in China, such as Sichuan cuisine, Guangdong cuisine, Hunan cuisine and so on.

中国有八大菜系，例如川菜、粤菜和湘菜等。

2. Sichuan cuisine is spicy, while Guangdong cuisine is light.

四川菜辣而广东菜清淡。

3. Maotai is one of the most famous liquor in China. It is very strong but it never goes to your head.

茅台是中国名酒之一。它烈但不上头。

中餐菜名 4 个翻译技巧

1. Cooking Method + Main Material + (with Accessories)
   烹饪方式 + 主料 +（with 辅料）
   例如：Stewed pork with salted vegetables 梅菜扣肉
2. Cooking Method + Main Material + in Seasoning
   烹饪方式 + 主料 + 调味料
   例如：Stewed pig hoof in clean soup 清炖猪蹄
3. Name/Place + Cooking Method + Main Material
   姓名 / 地点 + 烹饪方式 + 主料
   例如：Beijing roasted duck 北京烤鸭
4. Taste/Shape + Cooking Method + Main Material
   口味 / 形状 + 烹饪方式 + 主料
   例如：fragrant fried chicken 香煎鸡块

能力训练

情境 1：

Hanks 先生第一次来中国，餐厅服务员给 Hanks 先生及朋友介绍中国八大菜系并且推荐中国菜肴。

要求：以小组为单位总结出服务员的英文应对语句。

情境 2：

服务员到 Hanks 先生和朋友的雅间上菜，开始席间服务，介绍菜名、分菜、撤盘等。

要求：以小组为单位总结出服务员的英文应对语句。

项目3　The Food & Beverage（餐饮部）

学习任务4　Serving Western Food（西餐服务）

工作任务	Serving Western Food（西餐服务）	教学模式	线上线下混合教学模式 情境模拟教学模式
建议学时	4学时	教学地点	智慧教室或多媒体教室
任务描述	Hanks先生入住沈阳丽都索菲特酒店后，得知他的两个生意伙伴也在沈阳考察，提前约好几个朋友来酒店丽都西餐厅吃饭叙旧，顺便也品尝下酒店独特的西餐美味。		
学习目标	1. 掌握西餐点菜的服务程序及各个程序里常用的英文语句。 2. 掌握席间服务的流程及英文表达。 3. 能够准确无误地用英文描述西餐菜品。 4. 能够熟练地用英文做西餐服务。 5. 能够指导客人到酒店外的银行兑换外币。 6. 培养与他人团结协作的能力和有效沟通的能力。 7. 培养学生严谨敬业的工作作风		

头脑风暴

1. 你了解西餐的上菜顺序吗？
2. 你知道给客人点菜的服务流程是什么吗？
3. 如何给客人推荐菜肴呢？
4. 席间服务时如果客人不满意，该怎么处理？如何进行沟通？

词汇储备

西餐早餐

American Breakfast　美式早餐
English Breakfast　英式早餐
Continental Breakfast　欧陆式早餐（也称大陆式早餐）

饮料 Beverage

tea　茶　　　coca　可可　　　juice　果汁　　　fruit　水果　　　coffee　咖啡

肉类 Meat

ham　火腿　　　　　　　bacon　腌肉　　　　　　　sausage　香肠

面包 Bread

toast　烤面包（吐司）　　　croissant　牛角包　　　rolls　面包卷

sandwich 三明治   butter 黄油   jam 果酱

西餐上菜顺序

starter/appetizer 头盘

soup 汤

salad 色拉

entrée/main course 主菜

cheese/dessert 奶酪 / 甜点

coffee or tea 咖啡或茶

服务流程

西餐服务流程如下：

1. Greetings and handing the menu.
   问候客人并递上菜单。

2. Ordering and recommending the dishes.
   给客人推荐菜肴并点菜。

3. Confirming the dishes for the guest.
   给客人重复菜单。

4. Expressing the wishes.
   祝客人用餐愉快。

西餐服务

情境模拟

1. The first step: Greetings and handing the menu.
   第一步：问候客人并递上菜单。常用的句子有：

   a. Good afternoon evening, sir/madam/Mr. Wang...
      下午好，晚上好，先生、女士，王先生……

   b. Here's the menu.
      给您菜单。

   c. Here are the menu and wine list.
      给您菜单和酒单。

   d. You may have a look at it.
      您可以看一下。

   e. Please take your time.
      请您慢慢看。

   f. Are you ready to order now?
      您现在可以点餐了吗？

   g. Would you like to order now?
      您现在可以点餐了吗？

h. May I take your order now or you need another minute?
   您是现在点还是再等一会儿？

情境 1： 住店客人 Hanks 先生和朋友共 3 人来到酒店丽都西餐厅（Café Lido），想在此用午餐。
   Good morning, Mr. Hanks. What can I do for you?

情境 2： Smith 先生 1 人下午来到酒店丽都西餐厅（Café Lido）。
   Good afternoon, sir. May I help you?

2. The second step: ordering and recommending the dishes.
   第二步：给客人推荐菜肴并点菜。常用的句子有：

   a. Is there anything you can't eat? /Are you on a special diet?
      您有什么忌口的吗？

   b. Today's specialty is...
      今日特价菜是……

   c. May I suggest the...it's our house specialty/the latest recommendation/the latest style/chef's recommendation.
      招牌菜 / 最新推介 / 最新出品 / 厨师推荐

   d. Would you like to try...? What about...?
      您尝尝……菜？

   e. Would you like green tea or black tea?
      您喝绿茶还是红茶？

   f. What kind of drink would you like?
      您想喝什么？

   g. The broccoli is in season now, would you like to try it?
      西兰花是应季菜，您不点一个吗？

   h. It looks good, smells good and tastes good.
      它色香味俱全。

   i. It's very popular among the guest.
      这道菜深受欢迎。

   j. I am sure, you will like them.
      您一定会喜欢这道菜的。

   k. I'm afraid it will take some time to prepare.
      这个菜需较长时间准备。

   l. Anything else, please?
      您还需要别的吗？

情境 1：住店客人 Hanks 先生和朋友第一次来到丽都西餐厅，餐厅服务员给他推荐招牌菜。

Sir, fried foie gras, smoked salmon and Alaskan cod are our house specialty, would you like to try them?

情境 2：Smith 先生是酒店常客，餐厅服务员为他点餐。

Mr. Smith, today's specialty is French mushroom soup, it's very popular among the guest.

3. The third step: Confirming the dishes for the guest.
   第三步：给客人重复菜单。常用的句子有：
   a. So you'd like to have..., am I correct?
      您点了……，对吗？
   b. So that's..., anything else, please?
      您点了……，您还需要点别的吗？

情境 1：住店客人 Hanks 先生和朋友点了三份煎鹅肝、香熏三文鱼与阿拉斯加鳕鱼、榛果奶冻与巧克力塔。

Mr. Smith, you'd like to have three fried foie gras, smoked salmon and Alaskan cod, hazelnut jelly and chocolate tower. Am I correct?

情境 2：Smith 先生点了一份 T 骨牛排、法式蘑菇浓汤和蔬菜沙拉。

So that's a T-bone steak, French mushroom soup and vegetable salad, is that right, sir?

4. The fourth step: Expressing the wishes.
   第四步：祝客人用餐愉快。常用的句子有：
   a. Thank you, sir. Your dishes will be served in a minute.
      谢谢您，先生。您点的菜马上就好。
   b. Your order will be ready in a few minutes.
      您点的菜马上就好。祝您用餐愉快。
   c. Have a nice meal.
      祝您用餐愉快。
   d. I hope you have a wonderful evening.
      祝您用餐愉快。

能力进阶

客人对菜肴不满意，如何处理是一门技巧。

a. 首先道歉，安抚客人。

I'm awfully sorry.

b. 经领班同意，加菜或重新做。

This is oyster soup, compliment of our chef.

c. 表示感谢。

Thank you for bringing the matter to our attention.

语言使用

推荐常用的句型

a. Would you like to try...?

您尝试一下……，好吗？

b. How/what about...?

您尝试一下……，好吗？

c. Which flavor would you like, sweet or chilly?

您喜欢什么口味，辣的还是甜的？

d. Why not try...?

为什么不尝试一下……？

e. The spinach is in season now, would you like to try it?

菠菜是应季菜，您尝试一下？

f. It looks good, smells good and tastes good.

这道菜色香味俱全。

g. It's very popular among the guest.

这道菜很受欢迎。

h. I am sure, you will like them.

我相信您会喜欢。

能力训练

情境 1：

沈阳丽都索菲特酒店西餐厅服务员 Helen 给 Hanks 先生及朋友推荐本西餐厅特色菜肴。

要求：以小组为单位总结出服务员的英文应对语句。

情境 2：

Hanks 先生和朋友在用餐过程中，叫来服务员 Tom，生气地说："我要的牛排是五分熟，可是你们给我上的牛排是全熟的！"要求服务员重做。

要求：以小组为单位总结出服务员的英文应对语句。

学习任务 5　Bar Service（酒吧服务）

工作任务	Bar Service（酒吧服务）	教学模式	线上线下混合教学模式 情境模拟教学模式
建议学时	4学时	教学地点	智慧教室或多媒体教室
任务描述	Hanks 先生和朋友准备聚会，他们预订了该酒店二楼的丽贝屋法式小酒馆（La Bellevue Bistro Bar）雅间		
学习目标	1. 掌握酒吧里的设备用品及酒水名称。 2. 掌握酒吧服务程序常用的英文语句。 3. 能够熟练地用英文表达酒吧设备及酒水名称。 4. 能够用英文表达酒吧服务的常用语。 5. 能够准确无误地用英文描述中餐菜品。 6. 培养学生有效沟通的能力。 7. 培养学生正确的审美观、追求美好人生的性格		

头脑风暴

1. 酒店酒吧的工作任务有哪些？最基本的是哪一项？
2. 酒店酒吧有哪些常用设备？
3. 酒吧常用杯具的英文名称是什么？
4. 酒吧 menu 有哪几个部分？

词汇储备

酒吧常用设备

counter　吧台　　　　　　　　bar chair　酒吧椅　　　　　　corkscrew　酒钻
ice bucket　小冰桶　　　　　　ice maker　制冰机　　　　　　bottle opener　开瓶刀
cocktail shaker　调酒器　　　　pouring measure　量酒器　　　ice scoop　冰勺
juice extractor　果汁榨汁机　　electric blender　电动搅拌机

酒吧常用词汇

soft drink　软饮　　　　　　　soda water　苏打水　　　　　　whiskey　威士忌
vodka　伏特加　　　　　　　　brandy　白兰地　　　　　　　　gin　金酒
tequila　特基拉（龙舌兰）　　　rum　朗姆酒　　　　　　　　　liqueur　利口酒
on the rock　加冰块　　　　　　traight　不加冰　　　　　　　spirits　烈酒
cocktail　鸡尾酒　　　　　　　barman　酒吧男招待　　　　　　barmaid　酒吧女招待

服务流程

酒吧服务流程如下：

1. Greetings.
   问候，跟客人打招呼。
2. Leading the guest.
   为客人领位。
3. Taking orders and serving drinks.
   给客人介绍酒吧里的饮品，为客人点酒水并上酒水。
4. Expressing the wishes.
   表达祝愿。

酒吧服务

情境模拟

1. The first step: Greetings.
   第一步：问候。常用的句子有：
   a. Good evening, welcome to the bar.
      晚上好，欢迎光临我们酒吧。
   b. Good afternoon, how many people are there in your party?
      晚上好，您一共几位？

2. The second step: Leading the guest.
   第二步：为客人领位。常用的句子有：
   a. This way please.
      这边请。
   b. Mind your step.
      当心脚下。
   c. After me please.
      请跟我来。
   d. Would you prefer the smoking area or the non-smoking area?
      您想坐在吸烟区还是非吸烟区？
   e. Would you like to sit near the window or by the bar counter?
      您想坐在靠窗位置还是挨着吧台？

情境1：晚上9点，住店客人Hanks先生和朋友来到酒店二楼的丽贝屋法式小酒馆（La Bellevue Bistro Bar），他们想坐在靠窗位置。
Good evening, Mr. Hanks, welcome to Bistro Bar.
How many people are there in your party?

情境 2： 进店客人 Smith 先生下午来到酒店一楼回廊吧（Mezza Bar），他想坐在无烟区。
　　　　Good afternoon, sir. This way please.
　　　　Is this seat all right?

3. The third step: Taking orders and serving drinks.
   第三步：为客人点酒水并上酒水。常用的句子有：

   a. Good evening, may I take your order?
      晚上好，现在可以点酒水吗？

   b. (I'm) sorry to disturb you, but would you like to order now?
      抱歉打扰您，现在可以点酒水吗？

   c. I hope I haven't disturbed you...
      希望没打扰到您……

   d. Sorry to have taken up your time...
      抱歉占用您时间了……

   e. Would you like me to take your order?
      我现在可以为您点酒水吗？

   f. Would you mind me taking the cup away now?
      您介意我把杯子拿走吗？

情境 1： 晚上 9 点，住店客人 Hanks 先生和朋友来到酒店二楼的丽贝屋法式小酒馆（La Bellevue Bistro Bar），他们想喝当地啤酒，服务生做推荐。
　　　　Good evening, Mr. Hanks, welcome to Bistro Bar. We have fresh juices, soda water, beer and spirits. what would you like to drink? Xuehua beer is one of the most popular beer in Liaoning province. Would you like to have a try?

情境 2： 住店客人 Smith 先生下午来到酒店一楼回廊吧（Mezza Bar），点了一杯西瓜汁。
　　　　Good afternoon, sir. What about a glass of watermelon juice?

4. The fourth step: Expressing the wishes.
   第四步：表达祝愿。常用的句子有：

   a. Enjoy your drink.
      请享用！

   b. Please press the button if you need any help.
      如果您需要帮助，请按这个按钮。

   c. Please don't hesitate to let me know if you need any help.
      随时愿意为您效劳。

能力进阶

客人点的酒水本店里没有,此时如何向客人推荐合适的酒水就是一门技巧。

a. Sure, we've got three kinds of whiskey.
我们有三种威士忌。

b. I'm sorry that we don't have that cocktail.
抱歉,我们没有您要的那款鸡尾酒。

c. I'd like to recommend...
我想要推荐……

因酒店明确规定不允许服务生收取小费,委婉拒绝客人的技巧。

a. I'm sorry that we are not allowed to accept the tips.

b. Sorry, tips are not allowed here.
抱歉,酒店不允许我们收小费。

语言使用

酒店对客服务时经常会用到 Please don't hesitate to... 请随时……例如:

1. If I can do anything for you, please don't hesitate to let me know.
如果我能为您做些什么,请尽管说好了。

2. Please don't hesitate to call me if you need help.
需要帮忙的时候,请随时打电话给我。

3. If you need more information, please don't hesitate to let me know.
如果您需要更多的信息,请尽管说。

能力训练

情境 1:

服务员来到 Hanks 先生的餐桌,准备结账,这时客人准备给小费,但是该酒店明确规定不允许服务生收取小费,这时该如何拒绝?

要求:以小组为单位总结出服务员的英文应对语句。

情境 2:

Hanks 先生等人要求点一款酒吧酒水单上没有的鸡尾酒,服务员要问一下调酒师是否能调出这款鸡尾酒。

要求:以小组为单位总结出服务员的英文应对语句。

学习任务 6　Paying the Bill（餐厅结账服务）

工作任务	Paying the Bill（餐厅结账服务）	教学模式	线上线下混合教学模式 情境模拟教学模式
建议学时	2 学时	教学地点	智慧教室或多媒体教室
任务描述	Hanks 先生和朋友在沈阳丽都索菲特酒店乐轩华中餐厅（Sofitel Shenyang Lido Hotel）雅间用餐后，要求结账		
学习目标	1．熟练掌握用英文做结账服务的词汇。 2．掌握餐厅结账服务的流程。 3．掌握服务程序中常用的英文表达。 4．能够用英文准确无误地给客人结账。 5．能用英文回答客人对账单的疑问。 6．培养学生有效沟通的能力和解决问题的能力。 7．培养学生严谨敬业的工作作风		

头脑风暴

1．你了解餐厅结账的流程吗？
2．如何给客人解释账单？
3．你了解多少支付方式呢？

词汇储备

1．receipt　收据
2．change　零钱
3．service charge/service fee　服务费
4．charge　收费
5．bill　账单

服务流程

餐厅结账服务流程如下：

1．Giving the bill to the guests.
　　把账单交给客人。
2．Asking the guests how they would like to pay.
　　询问客人支付方式。

餐厅结账服务

项目 3　The Food & Beverage（餐饮部）

3. Giving the receipt or changes to the guests.
   把收据/零钱等交给客人。
4. Expressing the wishes.
   表达祝愿，希望客人再次光临。

情境模拟

1. The first step: Giving the bill to the guests.
   第一步：把账单给客人。常用的句子有：
   a. Here is the bill. Please check it.
      给您账单，请核对一下。
   b. Your bill totals...
      您一共消费……
2. The second step: Asking the guests how they would like to pay.
   第二步：询问客人的支付方式。常用的句子有：
   a. How would you like to pay, in cash or by credit card?
      您想如何支付，现金还是信用卡？
   b. How would you like to make the payment?
      您想如何支付？

情境 1：住店客人 Hanks 先生用完餐后，要求结账。
Good evening, Mr. Hanks. Here is the bill. Please check it.
How would you like to make the payment?

情境 2：Smith 先生在西餐厅用餐后，准备结账。
Good afternoon, sir. Your bill totals 672 Yuan RMB.
How would you like to pay, in cash or by credit card?

3. The third step: Giving the receipt or changes to the guests.
   第三步：把收据/零钱等给客人。常用的句子有：
   a. Here is the receipt.
      给您收据。
   b. Here is the change.
      给您零钱。

情境 1：Hanks 先生结账时跟服务员说要记入房账，服务员让 Hanks 先生在收据上签字。
Mr. Hanks, we will charge it to your room account. Please sign your name and room number here.

情境 2：Smith 先生拿出 680 元人民币结账，服务员把找零的 8 元递给他。
Here is the change for you, 8 Yuan RMB, sir.

4. The fourth step: Expressing the wishes.
   第四步：表达祝愿。常用的句子有：

   a. (I) hope you did enjoy your meal here.
      希望您用餐愉快。
   b. Welcome to come again.
      欢迎您下次光临。
   c. Welcome to be with us again.
      欢迎您下次光临。

能力进阶

如果遇到客人质疑账单的情况，跟客人解释账单。常用的句子有：

a. What seems to be the mistake, sir?
   哪个地方有不对吗，先生？
b. I'm terribly sorry. Would you mind checking it again?
   很抱歉，您介意再检查一下吗？
c. Well, that's all right this time. We charge 10% service charge.
   这次正确，我们有 10% 服务费的。

客人对账单
有异议

语言使用

Would you like 主要用法

1. Would you like +sth.

   e.g.: Would you like some fruit? (=Do you want some fruit?)
   您想吃些水果吗？

2. Would you like +to do sth.

   e.g.: Would you like to drink a cup of coffee? (=Do you want to drink a cup of coffee?)
   您想喝杯咖啡吗？

3. Would you like +sb.to do sth.

   e.g.: Would you like me to confirm it? (=Do you want me to confirm it?)
   您想要我再核对一下吗？

拓展知识：对于"Would you like..."提出的建议或要求，肯定回答常用"Yes, please."或"Yes, I would love like to."，否定回答常用"No, thanks."。

能力训练

情境1：

Hanks 先生和朋友来到西餐厅用餐后，要求结账。服务员拿来账单后，客人说自己现金不够了，问能否用信用卡结账。

要求：以小组为单位总结出服务员的英文应对语句，注意服务礼仪。

可以使用以下方式表达：

a. Excuse me, sir. You have to change US dollars into RMB at the exchange counter over there.

打扰了，先生，您可以去那边的外币兑换柜台，把美元兑换成人民币。

b. I'm sorry. I am afraid we don't accept traveler's check.

抱歉，恐怕我们酒店不能使用旅行者支票。

c. What credit card are you holding?

您使用什么信用卡？

情境2：

Hanks 先生和朋友来到西餐厅用餐后，要求结账。服务员拿来账单后，给客人解释账单情况；但是客人认为账单有误，认为酒店多收了自己的钱。

要求：以小组为单位总结出服务员的英文应对语句。

学习任务 7　Handling Complaints（处理投诉）

工作任务	Handling Complaints（处理投诉）	教学模式	线上线下混合教学模式 情境模拟教学模式
建议学时	2 学时	教学地点	智慧教室或多媒体教室
任务描述	Miller 夫人是刚入住酒店的旅行团一员，在办理入住过程中，她的行李丢失了，现在她已经在房间等了半个小时，还没等到她的行李，她非常生气，打电话向礼宾部投诉		
学习目标	1. 能听懂客人关于客房、餐饮方面的投诉。 2. 掌握处理投诉六个步骤。 3. 掌握每个步骤的英文表达。 4. 能够处理餐饮投诉及处理醉酒客人。 5. 培养学生发现问题和解决问题的能力。 6. 培养学生有效沟通的能力。		

头脑风暴

1. 您能陈述处理投诉的流程吗？
2. 在酒店的不同部门，你会如何处理投诉呢？
3. 如果酒吧有一位醉酒的客人，您将如何处理？

词汇储备

1. complain　*v.* 投诉，抱怨　complaint　*n.* 投诉，抱怨
2. deal with the complaint　处理投诉
3. handle the complaint　处理投诉
4. apologize　*v.* 抱歉
5. apology　*n.* 抱歉　make an apology
6. inconvenient　*adj.* 不方便的
7. inconvenience　*n.* 不方便
8. on the house　免费

服务流程

处理投诉流程如下：

1. Listening to the guest carefully.
   倾听客人陈述。

2. Making an apology.
   表示抱歉。
3. Giving explanation.
   给出解释。
4. Offering help.
   向客人提出帮助解决的办法。
5. Taking action.
   立刻采取行动帮助客人解决。
6. Giving feedback.
   给出反馈内容。

处理投诉

处理投诉六步骤

情境模拟

处理投诉流程及句子表达如下：

1. The first step: Listening to the guest carefully.
   第一步：倾听客人陈述。常用的句子有：
   a. May I know what's wrong?
      能告诉我发生了什么事吗？
   b. Would you tell me what has happened?
      能告诉我发生了什么事吗？

2. The second step: Making an apology.
   第二步：表示抱歉。常用的句子有：
   a. I do apologize.
      我真的很抱歉。
   b. We make an apology for the inconvenience.
      给您带来的不便向您道歉。
   c. Please relax. Madam, I will try to help.
      女士，请你冷静一下，我们一定尽力解决。
   d. There could have been some mistakes. I do apologize.
      如果有什么不对的地方，我真的很抱歉。
   e. It's obviously our mistake.
      很明显是我们的错误。

3. The third, fourth and fifth step:
   Giving explanation.
   Offering help.
   Taking action.
   第三、四、五步：给出解释，向客人提出帮助解决办法，立刻采取行动帮助客人解决。常用的句子有：

a. Our repairman will come to your room in 10 minutes.

我们的修理工 10 分钟就到您的房间。

b. I will send some one up to your room to fix it at once.

我们立刻派人过去给您修理。

c. I am sure this will not happen again.

我们保证，下次不会再发生此事。

d. The housemaid will bring some other pillows and slippers soon.

客房服务员会马上给您拿多余的枕头和拖鞋。

4. The sixth step: Giving feedback.

第六步：给出反馈内容。常用的句子有：

a. We might overlook some details. Thank you for bringing the matter to our attention.

我们可能忽略了某些细节，谢谢您让我们对此事引起注意。

b. If there is anything else I can do for you, please don't hesitate to call me.

如果还有什么需要我为您做的，请给我打电话。

能力进阶

看一看，更了解

M: Manager; G: Guest

M: Good evening, sir. I'm the manager. How may I help you?

G: I ordered a medium-rare steak. It was overdone and is almost uneatable.

M: Oh, I'm very sorry, sir. We'll prepare another one for you at once. Please wait a few minutes.

G: Well, there's something else. I asked the waitress to bring me another fork, but she ignored my request.

M: I'm sure the waitress didn't mean to be rude. She just began working a week ago and still doesn't understand much English. I'll bring you a fork immediately and be right back.

(Minutes later...)

M: Here's your fork, sir. This is a chef's salad; it's on the house.

G: Thank you.

M: Please take your time and enjoy yourself. Sorry again for the inconvenience. I assure you it won't happen again.

(R: Receptionist; G: Guest)

R: Good morning, Ms. Black. How may I help you?

G: I am afraid I have a complaint. My room is too damp. I'd like a room facing south and full of sunlight.

R: Please wait a moment, Ms. Black. Let me check... Will Room 1018 be all right? It's facing south and very comfortable.

G: Can I be on the eighth floor? My friend is in Room 803.

R: I'm sorry, Ms. Black. The rooms on the eighth floor are full.

G: Well, it seems I'll have to take Room 1018. Whats the room rate?

R: It's the same rate as Room 615.

G: Can I see Room 1018 before I move in?

R: Of course, Ms. Black. I will send a bellboy up with the key.

G: That's very kind of you.

R: If you like Room 1018, the bellboy can help you move your things immediately.

G: Thank you very much.

语言使用

条件状语从句

1. 引导词：if（如果），unless（除非，如果不），as long as（除非，只要），supposing（假设），in case（如果）。

2. 分类：

（1）第一类：真实条件句。主句用一般将来时的时候，条件状语从句用一般现在时或现在完成时。

a. I'll not move unless you make sure everything is OK.
   除非你确信一切正常，否则我不会离开。

b. You will have the table if you book it in advance.
   如果您提前预订，您可以在这个餐桌用餐。

c. I shall not report it to your manager if you agree to the solution.
   如果你同意这个解决方案，我就不会向你的经理汇报。

（2）第二类：条件状语从句。在虚拟语气中使用。

虚拟语气	If+ 从句	主句
与现在事实相反	be—were 动词—过去式	would, should, could, might + 动词原形
与过去事实相反	had+ 动词过去分词	would, should, could, might+have + 动词过去分词
与将来事实相反	were to + 动词原形 should + 动词原形	would, should, could, might + 动词原形

a. If I had enough money, I would reserve a presidential suite.
   如果我有足够的钱，我会预订一个总统套房。

b. If I had known your response, I would not have been so angry with the manager.
   如果我知道你的反应，我就不会跟经理这么生气了。

c. If you were to leave tomorrow, I would arrange everything for you.
   如果您打算明天离开，我会把一切都为您安排好。

(3) 条件状语从句中的省略：从句的部分可以省略倒装，把 if 省掉，助动词提前。如：

a. Had I enough money, I would reserve a presidential suite.
   如果我有足够的钱，我会预订一个总统套房。

b. Had I known your response, I would not have been so angry with the manager.
   如果我知道你的反应，我就不会跟经理这么生气了。

c. Were you to leave tomorrow, I would arrange everything for you.
   如果您打算明天离开，我会把一切都为您安排好。

练一练

用所给单词的正确形式填空。

1. Unless it _____ (rain), we will not change our plan.

2. If you _____ (come) earlier, please remember to clean the room.

3. The manager will be very angry if you _____ (tell) him the news later.

4. We will keep the car space for you if you _____ (pay) a deposit here.

5. The customer will feel satisfied if he _____ (get) his return ticket.

能力训练

情境 1：

两人一组编排对话：Hanks 先生给 room service 打电话，订好的早餐，现在还没有送到房间。

要求：两人一组，完成对话，注意服务礼仪。

情境 2：

Miller 女士的房间不太舒服，她投诉说房间太潮湿了，她想要换一间朝阳并且在八楼的房间，这样能和她的朋友住同一层。

要求：两人一组，完成对话，注意服务礼仪。

能力拓展

餐饮服务英语 200 句

1. Good morning, Chinese Restaurant. How can I help you?
   早上好，中餐厅，有什么需要帮助的吗？

2. For how many people, and when would you like to book?
   订几个人的餐，您订在什么时候？

3. For how many people, and when will you be coming?
   订几个人的餐，您什么时候来？

4. Just a moment, please. I'll check the availability for you.
   请稍后，我来为您查查是否有空。

5. Let me check if we have any vacancy.
   让我来查看一下是否有空位。

6. Would you like a table in the hall or a private room?

   您喜欢大厅里的餐台还是要一个包间？

7. What time would you like to book your table?

   您要订在什么时间？

8. What time would you like your table?

   您什么时间就餐？

9. May I know your name and your room number?

   请告诉我您的名字和房间号。

10. May I have your name and your phone number?

    请告诉我您的名字和电话号码。

11. May I have your name, please?

    请告诉我您的名字。

12. You are welcome. We look forward to your coming tomorrow. Thank you for your calling.

    不用谢。我们恭候您明天光临。谢谢您的来电。

13. We look forward to having you with us。

    我们期待您明天前来就餐。

14. We have three east private rooms, but each of them can be seated for eleven at most. We have a private room facing south. It can be seated fifteen people. This private room is called Starwood.

    酒店有三个东包间，但每一间最多能坐 11 位。我们还有一个包间向南。里面能坐 14 位，这个包间叫作星木。

15. What is it going to be, the Chinese food or the Western food?

    您要吃中餐还是西餐？

16. Would you like to have a la carte or table d'hote?

    你们是要点菜还是吃套餐？

17. By the way, the minimum charge for a private room in the evening is required 200 Yuan per person.

    顺便说一声，晚上包间每位最低消费为 200 元。

18. In whose name is the reservation made?

    以谁的名字预订？

19. I'm afraid the tables in the hall have been fully booked for that time. But we still have a few private rooms. Would you like to have a private room?

    恐怕那个时间的大厅餐台已经订满了，我们还有几个包间。您看包间怎么样？

20. I'm afraid all our tables have been taken.

    恐怕我们已经客满。

21. I'm afraid the tables have been fully booked for that time. Would you like to make the reservation at another time?

恐怕那个时间的餐台已经订满了。您是否可以换个时间？

22．I'm afraid we are fully booked for that moment. It's the busy season/ hot season/peak season, you know.

恐怕那个时间的餐台已经订满了。您知道那是在高峰期。

23．Would you like to make a reservation at another time?

您能否换个时间？

24．Is it possible for you to change the time?

您是否可以换个时间呢？

25．Good afternoon, sir. Welcome to our restaurant. May I help you?

下午好，先生，需要我为您服务吗？

26．How many tables shall we arrange?

请问我们应该安排多少张餐台呢？

27．How many tables would you like?

您需要多少张餐台？

28．How would you like us to arrange the tables?

您喜欢我们怎么摆放餐台呢？

29．How would you like us to set up the banquets?

您希望我们如何安排宴会？

30．How much would you like to spend per head?

您想每位消费多少？

31．What drinks are you going to have?

用什么酒水？

32．Could you have any special demands for the banquet menu?

您对宴会菜单有什么特别的要求？

33．We serve Cantonese, Sichuan, Shanghai and Beijing Cuisines, which cuisine would you prefer?

我们有粤菜、川菜、沪菜和京菜，您喜欢哪一种呢？

34．The four major Chinese cuisines are Shandong Cuisine, Guangdong Cuisine, Sichuan Cuisine and Huaiyang Cuisine. Generally speaking, Shandong Cuisine is heavy, Guangdong Cuisine is light, but Sichuan Cuisine is spicy and hot. Huaiyang Cuisine is famous for its cutting technique and original flavor.

这四种主要的中国菜系是山东菜、广东菜、四川菜和淮扬菜。一般来说，山东菜味重香浓，广东菜清淡可口，四川菜麻辣浓香。淮扬菜则以刀工和原味而闻名。

35．How about Huaiyang Cuisine?

淮扬菜怎么样？

36．How would you like to pay for the banquets?

请问宴会怎样付款？

37. How about the deposit?
    怎样交押金？

38. We'll get everything ready in advance.
    我们会准备好一切。

39. Is there anything else I can do for you?
    还有什么需要我做的吗？

40. My name is Wang Qian. If you have anything, please call me. We look forward to your arrival.
    我叫王倩，有事情打电话给我，我们恭候您的光临。

餐厅服务

41. Good evening, sir. Have you made a reservation?
    晚上好，先生，您有预订吗？

42. How many persons, please?
    请问几位？

43. We were expecting you.
    我们正在恭候您的光临。

44. A table for six?
    一张六人桌吗？

45. Is it only three of you?
    就你们三位吗？

46. Could you follow me, please?
    请跟我来，好吗？

47. Please come this way.
    请这边走。

48. Where would you like to sit?
    您喜欢坐哪儿？

49. Please choose table as you like.
    请随便坐。

50. Will this table be all right?
    这张桌子行吗？

51. How about this table?
    这张桌子怎么样？

52. You may sit where you like.
    您可以随便坐。

53. I'm sorry, this table is already reserved.
    对不起，这张桌子已经有人预订了。

54. You've booked a table for four people. Is that right?
    您预订了六人台位，对吗？

55. I'm afraid that the table you reserved is not ready yet.
    恐怕您预订的餐台还没有准备好。

56. I'll show you to your table. This way, please. This is your table. Will this table all right?
    我带您到您的餐台去，请这边走，这是您的餐台。这张桌子可以吗？

57. I'm afraid this table is reserved for 7 p.m.
    恐怕这个餐台已经有人预订了，7点就来。

58. There will be a wait of about twenty minutes.
    您大概要等上20分钟。

59. Would you mind sharing a table?
    您介意与别人共用一张桌子吗？

60. You can sit over there if you like and we'll call you when we have a table.
    如果您愿意，您可以坐在那边等一会儿，有餐台的时候我们就会通知您。

61. I'm afraid that we let another guest sit at your table since you did not arrive at the reserved time.
    因为您没有按照预订的时间来，所以我们将座位安排给另一位客人了。

62. Would you mind waiting until it is available or would you prefer another table?
    您介意等一会儿吗？或者您去另一桌，好吗？

63. We can seat you very soon.
    我们很快就会安排您入座。

64. Could you wait for another five minutes, please?
    请再等五分钟，好吗？

65. It may take about 15 minutes.
    可能需要15分钟。

66. I'm sorry to have kept you waiting.
    很抱歉让您久等了。

67. Do you have a meal voucher /breakfast voucher?
    您有餐券或早餐券吗？

68. Take your seat, please. /Please be seated.
    请坐。

69. Would you like a high chair for your child?
    要不要给您的孩子拿一张高椅子呢？

70. I'll bring you the menu. /I'll get you the menu.
    我给您拿菜单来。

71. Here is the menu.
    这是菜单。

72. What would you like to order?
    您想要点什么？

73. May I have your order now?
    您现在点菜吗?

74. Are you ready to order now?
    您准备点菜吗?

75. Would you like to order now?
    您现在想点菜吗?

76. Have you decided what you'd like?
    您决定吃什么菜了吗?

77. What would you like to start with?
    您想先来点什么?

78. Will you dine a la carte or take table d'hote?
    您点菜还是套餐?

79. We have both buffet-style and a la carte dishes, which would you prefer?
    我们有自助式和点菜式,您喜欢哪一种?

80. We serve breakfast from seven to nine in the morning.
    我们从早上7点到9点提供早餐。

81. What kind of breakfast do you want to have, Continental or American?
    您想吃哪一种早餐,大陆式还是美式?

82. Would you like to try our house specials?
    您想尝尝我们的特色菜吗?

83. Would you like to have a try?
    您想尝试一下吗?

84. Which flavor would you prefer, sweet or chilly?
    您喜欢什么口味,甜口还是辣味?

85. How would you like your steak done, sir, rare, medium or well-done?
    您希望我们怎样做您点的牛排(牛排要几分熟),半生、中等还是全熟?

86. What would you like to go with your steak?
    您点的牛排要搭配什么吃?

87. Are you on a special diet?
    您对饮食有特别要求吗?

88. We offer special menus for different diets.
    我们有特殊食谱,可以满足不同的饮食需要。

89. We have a wide range of vegetarian dishes for you to choose from.
    我们有许多素菜可供您选择。

90. Would you like to go over the wine list?
    您看一下酒水单好吗?

91. Would you like your beer draught or bottled?

您喜欢扎啤还是瓶装啤酒？

92. How about Yanjing Beer? It's very popular here.
    燕京啤酒怎么样？在这里很受欢迎。

93. This wine is only served by the bottle. How about...? It's served by the glass.
    这种酒我们只按瓶出售。……（另一种酒）怎么样？我们可以按杯出售。

94. With ice or without ice, sir?
    先生，请问是否要加冰呢？

95. Would you like something to drink?
    您想喝点什么？

96. It's served by the dozen.
    它是按打卖的。

97. Shall I bring your coffee now or later?
    我是现在为您上咖啡还是迟些时候上呢？

98. How about the dessert?
    来点儿甜点吗？

99. Anything for dessert?
    需要甜点吗？

100. May I show you the dessert menu?
     您要看看甜点菜单吗？

101. What soup would you prefer?
     您喜欢什么汤？

102. We have clear soup and cream soup at your choice.
     我们有清汤和奶油汤供您选择。

103. The chef's special is shrimp with crispy fried rice crust.
     厨师的拿手菜是虾仁锅巴。

104. Many guests give high comments on it.
     很多顾客对这道菜都给予了很高的评价。

105. What kind of dressing would you like on your salad?
     请问您喜欢哪一种色拉酱？

106. What would you like for your main course?
     主菜吃什么？

107. I can recommend roast beef.
     我可以推荐烤牛肉。

108. I would suggest crispy fried duck.
     我建议您点香酥鸭。

109. Shrimp salad is being served today.
     今天供应虾仁色拉。

110. Roast duck is the specialty here, I should say.
我想说烤鸭是这里的特色菜。

111. These are our local specials.
这些是我们的地方特色菜。

112. What would you like to go with your main course?
主菜配什么吃？

113. What kind of dressing?
要哪种酱汁？

114. Shall I bring you a knife and fork?
您需不需要刀叉呢？

115. Anything else?
还需要别的吗？

116. Would you like to try today's special?
您想尝尝今天的特色菜吗？

117. Today's special is Crisp Fried Spareribs with a 40% discount.
今天的特价菜是香酥排骨。有6折优惠。

118. It's crisp/tasty/tender/clear/strong/spicy/aromatic.
它很酥脆/可口/鲜嫩/清淡/浓烈/辣/香味扑鼻。

119. It's a well-known delicacy in Chinese Cuisine.
它是中国菜的一道有名的佳肴。

120. You'll love it.
您会喜欢的。

121. It's for four persons.
这道菜是四人份。

122. It's out of season.
这个已经过季了。

123. The beef BBQ is terrific.
牛肉烧烤可是棒极了。

124. If you are in a hurry, I would recommend...
如果您赶时间，我推荐您……

125. It will stimulate your appetite.
它会让您开胃的。

126. This is very hot. Please be careful.
这道菜很烫，请小心。

127. This food is best eaten while hot.
这道菜最好趁热吃。

128. May I serve it to you now?

现在可以上菜了吗？

129. Please wait a moment. Your order will be here soon.
请稍等，您的餐点马上送到。

130. Your meal will be ready soon.
您点的菜很快就好。

131. I'll repeat your order: Fried Mandarin Fish in Squirrel Shape, Dongpo Pork, Sugar Candy Lotus Seeds, Fried Prawns with pepper Salt, Eggplant with Garlic sauce, Stir Fry Gourd with Garlic and Yanjing Beer.
我重复一下您点的东西：松鼠鳜鱼、东坡肉、冰糖湘莲、椒盐炸明虾、鱼香茄子、芙蓉炒丝瓜和燕京啤酒。

132. This is your last dish. Please enjoy.
菜齐了，请慢用。

133. Excuse me, may I take your plate?
打搅了，我可以把盘子撤掉吗？

134. Shall I change this plate with a smaller one?
我把这个换成小一点的碟子好吗？

135. May I move this plate to the side?
我可以把这个碟子移到一边去吗？

136. May I clear the table for you?
我可以为您收拾桌子吗？

137. I am terribly sorry. Is there anything I can do for you?
太抱歉了，我能为您做点什么吗？

138. I seem to have brought the wrong dish. I'll get you another one.
我好像上错了一个菜。我再为您重上一个。

139. It is free of charge.
这个是免费的。

140. It is complimentary./ That would be on the house.
这是免费奉送的。

141. How would you like to make your payment? It totals 566 Yuan.
请问怎样付款？一共是 566 元。

142. How would you like to pay? We accept cash and credit card.
您想怎样付款？我们接受现金和信用卡。

143. One bill or separate bills?
是合单还是分开付账？

144. I'm afraid we don't accept traveler's checks.
恐怕我们不收旅行支票。

145. I'm afraid we don't accept tips. It's against our regulations. Thank you all the same.

恐怕我们不收小费，这是违反规定的，谢谢。

146．Please sign your name here. Here is your card.
请在这里签名，这是您的卡。

147．Here is your bill. The total is 566 Yuan including 10% service charge.
这是您的账单，一共 566 元，包括 10% 的服务费。

148．Sure, we'll charge it to your room bill, and your room number is 3998，is that right? Please sign your name here.
好的，我们会加在您的房间账单上的，您的房间号码是 3998，对吗？请您在这儿签字。

149．Here is your change. Please check it.
这是找您的钱。请核对一下。

150．May I introduce some typical Chinese food to you?
需要我为您介绍一下地道的中国菜吗？

151．Are you satisfied with your food?
您吃的还满意吗？

152．Would you like green tea or black tea?
您是喝绿茶还是红茶？

153．Is everything to your satisfaction?
一切还满意吗？

154．We hope to serve you again soon.
欢迎您再来。

155．We hope we'll have another opportunity to serve you soon.
我们期待下次能为您效劳。

酒吧服务

156．Would you prefer smoking area or non-smoking area?
您想坐在吸烟区还是无烟区？

157．This way please. Mind your step.
请这边走，小心脚下。

158．Would you like to sit near the window or by the bar counter?
您想坐在窗边还是挨着吧台？

159．Would you like local beer or imported beer?
想要当地啤酒还是进口的？

160．We have orange, pineapple, grapefruit, mango, peach and tomato juice.
有鲜橙、菠萝、葡萄、杧果、桃和番茄汁。

161．Sorry to have kept you waiting. Here is your beer and mango juice. Would you like anything else?
让您久等了。您的燕京啤酒和芒果汁。还要其他的吗？

162. You are welcome. Please enjoy your drink.
 不客气，请您慢用。

163. How do you like your coffee, with milk and sugar?
 您喜欢什么样的咖啡，要加牛奶和糖吗？

164. Do you like your tea strong or weak?
 您喜欢茶浓点还是淡点？

165. Would you like it now or after dinner?
 您想现在上还是餐后上？

166. How would you like it, straight or on the rocks?
 您想怎么喝，加不加冰？

167. What can I make for you tonight?
 今晚需要我为您调制什么酒？

168. You can hold the payment of the bill until you decide to leave if you like.
 您可以在离开前结账。

169. This kind of wine is strong.
 这种酒酒性很烈。

170. This wine is usually popular with ladies.
 这种酒通常适合女士的口味。

171. With iced water, not with ice. Ice will spoil the taste.
 只加冰水不加冰，冰会破坏味道。

172. Would you like to try some Chinese alcohol?
 您想不想试一试中国酒呢？

173. It's rather strong but never goes to the head.
 它度数较高但是从不上头。

174. Have you decided what you'd like to drink?
 您决定喝什么？

175. Which vintage would you prefer?
 您喜欢哪一种葡萄酒？

176. "Mao Tai" is the best Chinese spirit.
 茅台是一种很好的中国白酒。

177. How about champagne?
 香槟怎么样？

178. Would you like to have some snacks with your wine?
 您要不要叫一点小吃来下酒呢？

179. Here is the wine list.
 这是酒水牌。

180. We have a very extensive cellar.

我们的藏酒非常丰富。

181. I'll put the cork here.
 我把软木塞放在这儿。

182. You are welcome. Enjoy your drink.
 不客气，请您享用吧。

183. Please tell me when.
 如果够了请告诉我（倒酒时）。

184. How is the taste/color/bouquet/temperature/... of the wine?
 酒的味道/颜色/香味/温度如何？

投诉

185. I'll speak to the person in charge and ask him to take care of the problem.
 我会对负责人讲，让他来处理这件事。

186. Please calm down, sir, I'll try to help you.
 先生请您冷静，我会尽力帮助您的。

187. Please relax, madam. I will take care of it according to your request.
 请放心，夫人，我将按您的要求办。

188. I'll have them make you another one.
 我叫他们再给您换一份。

189. I'm terribly sorry, sir. Would you like it cooked a little more?
 实在对不起，先生，您想把它再煮一下吗？

190. Would you like something else while you are waiting?
 您在等的时候还要点什么别的吗？

191. I'm sorry, sir. Do you mind trying something else? That would be on the house, of course.
 对不起，先生。您换点别的可以吗？当然，这是不收费的。

192. I'm sorry it's not to your taste. I will take it back to the chef.
 我很抱歉这不合您的胃口，我现在就把它拿到厨师长那儿去。

193. I am sorry for our miscalculation.
 我为我们的误算感到抱歉。

194. Thank you for telling us about it, sir, I'll look into the matter at once.
 感谢您为我们提供这些情况，先生，我马上调查此事。

195. Sorry, we'll look into this matter.
 对不起，我们会调查这件事的。

196. Could you tell me what the problem is?
 您可以告诉我有什么问题吗？

197. I'm awfully sorry for my carelessness.
 对于我的粗心我非常抱歉。

198. Sorry, sir, I will solve the problem for you as soon as possible.

对不起先生,我会尽快为您解决这个问题的。

199. I'm sure the waiter didn't mean to be rude. Perhaps he didn't understand you correctly. I do apologize for it.

非常抱歉,先生。我相信我们的服务员不是有意的。可能他不是很明白您的意思。

200. I'm awfully sorry for the error, sir. This is the cold beer you ordered and this is and extra plate of popcorn. I hope you enjoy it.

对这个错误我感到非常抱歉。这是您要的冰镇啤酒。这是一盘额外的爆米花。希望您喜欢。

项目 4

The Fitness Center（康乐部）

学习任务 1　Gym Service（健身房服务）

工作任务	Gym Service （健身房服务）	教学模式	线上线下混合教学模式 情境模拟教学模式
建议学时	4学时	教学地点	智慧教室或多媒体教室
任务描述	Hanks先生等一行七人入住沈阳丽都索菲特酒店后，对酒店提供的接待、餐饮及商务服务都非常满意。 　　在酒店入住期间，客人们去健身中心健身，作为健身房的服务人员，应该如何接待他们？应该掌握什么样的基本知识和技巧？		
学习目标	1. 了解酒店康乐部主要健身项目。 2. 掌握酒店康乐部服务接待程序及各个程序的英文表达。 3. 了解健身房主要工作任务。 4. 培养学生敬业严谨的工作作风。		

头脑风暴

1. 酒店健身房都有哪些设施？英文怎么说？
2. 如果你是酒店健身房服务员，给客人服务的服务程序是什么，各个程序应如何与客人进行英语沟通？
3. 如果客人有不了解的服务项目，怎么用英语与客人沟通？

词汇储备

1. locker　寄物柜
2. stationary bicycle　健身自行车
3. treadmill/jogging machine　跑步机
4. weight-lifting machine　举重机
5. billiards room　台球室
6. tennis court　网球场
7. gymnasium　（缩写：gym）　健身房，体育馆
8. massage　按摩
9. sauna　桑拿
10. barbell　杠铃
11. golf course　高尔夫球场
12. warm up　热身
13. stretch　伸展动作
14. aerobics　有氧操
15. boxing　拳击
16. karate　空手道
17. rowing machine　划船机
18. dumbbell　哑铃
19. yoga　瑜伽
20. lose weight　减重
21. gain weight　增重
22. build muscle　增强肌肉
23. shape your body　塑身
24. coach/trainer　教练
25. fat　脂肪
26. scale　秤

服务流程

健身房服务流程如下：

1. Greeting the guests.
   问候。
2. Asking the guest if they need any help.
   询问客人是否需要帮忙。
3. Introducing the services.
   向客人介绍健身房服务项目。
4. Expressing the wishes.
   表达祝愿。

情境模拟

1. The first step: Greetings.
   第一步：问候。常用的句子有：
   a. Good morning/afternoon/evening, sir/madam/Miss.
      上午/下午/晚上好/先生/女士。
   b. Are you the guest of our hotel, sir?
      先生，您是我们酒店的住店客人吗？
   c. Could you please show us your room card/member card to register?
      您能告诉我们您的房卡/会员卡以便登记吗？
   d. Could you please sign your name here?
      请您在这里签名，好吗？
2. The second step: Asking the guest if they need any help.
   第二步：询问客人是否需要帮忙。常用的句子有：
   a. Do you need the safe-deposit service?
      您需要保险箱服务吗？
   b. This is the key to the locker.
      给您更衣室的钥匙。
   c. Please keep it well. Locker room is over there. Lady's is on the right and gentleman's is on the left.
      请您保管好钥匙。更衣室在那边，女士在右侧，男士在左侧。
   d. Sir/Miss, Excuse me. The health club will be closed in 5 minutes.
      先生/女士，打扰了，健身俱乐部5分钟内关闭。
   e. We supply service to the our hotel guests and the club members and their friends.
      我们为住店客人和俱乐部会员及他们的朋友提供服务。
3. The third step: Introducing the services.
   第三步：向客人介绍健身房服务项目。常用的句子有：
   a. We have a well-equipped keep-fit gym with all the latest fitness apparatus, such as...
      我们有设施完善的健身房，里面有最新的娱乐运动器械，如……

b. We also have facilities like a billiards room and a very big indoor swimming pool.
我们也有像保龄球室和室内游泳池这样的设施。

c. We have an exercise room for Taijiquan and Qigong. If you're interested in them you can go and learn from the resident coach there.
我们这里有练习太极拳和气功的房间。如果您感兴趣，可以去跟那里的长驻教练学习一下。

情境：Miller 女士是沈阳索菲特酒店的住店客人，晚餐后，她来到健身房咨询健身项目。

Fitness Center attendant: Good evening, madam, welcome to our Fitness Center.
Guest: Good evening. I am here to know something about your Fitness Center.
Fitness Center attendant: Yes, we have facilities like a billiard room, bowling alley and a very big indoor swimming pool and a sauna.
Guest: Do you have any exercise equipments?
Fitness Center attendant: Sure, we have weight-lifting machines, rowing machines and jogging machines.
Guest: When is your Fitness Center open?
Fitness Center attendant: It's open from 9:00 a.m. to 11:00 p.m.

4. Expressing the wishes.
表达祝愿。常用的句子有：

a. Have a good evening.
晚安。

b. Please contact us if you need any help.
如果您需要帮助，请联系我。

c. Please don't hesitate to let me know if you need any help.
如果您需要帮助，请联系我。

d. Look forward to seeing you again.
期待再次见面。

e. Thank you for coming.
感谢光顾。

能力进阶

健身房服务过程中的特殊情况下，服务程序及常用的句子有：
询问客人是否是住店客人

Are you the guest of our hotel, sir/madam?
先生/女士，您是我们酒店的住店客人吗？

项目 4　The Fitness Center（康乐部）

请求客人签名

a. Could you please sign your name here?
   请您在这里签名可以吗？

b. Would you mind signing your name here?
   请您在这里签名可以吗？

c. Please sign your name here.
   请您在这里签名。

请客人出示房卡登记

a. Could you please show us your room card to register?
   请出示您的房卡登记，可以吗？

b. Could you please show us your member card to register?
   请出示您的会员卡登记，可以吗？

为客人介绍（解释）健身会员卡

a. The member card for swim is RMB 700 Yuan for 30 times and available in 3 months.
   游泳会员卡 30 次 700 元人民币，3 个月内有效。

b. The member card for gym is RMB 900 Yuan for 40 times and available in 2 months.
   健身房会员卡 40 次 900 元，2 个月内有效。

向客人说明健身房的使用须知和危险提示，常用的句子有：

a. Excuse me, sir/Miss, it's mot allowed to go in the gym wearing swimsuit.
   抱歉，先生/女士，穿泳衣不允许进入健身房。

b. You can do exercises in gym if you put on the sports shoes and suits.
   如果您穿上运动服和运动鞋的话您可以在健身房锻炼。

c. We prepared all kinds of machines for you.
   我们为您准备了各式各样的健身器材。

d. It's free of charge.
   这是免费的。

e. A cup of cold coffee and a coke. Wait for a moment please.
   一杯冰咖啡和一罐可乐。请稍等。

f. May I smoke here? Yes, I'll take the ashtray for you.
   我可以在这里吸烟吗？可以，我把烟灰缸给您拿来。

g. The swimming pool and the equipment are free for our hotel guests.
   游泳池和器械对于住店客人是免费的。

h. We supply the bath towel, shampoo, bath foam for free.
   我们免费提供毛巾、洗发露和浴液。

i. The indoor swimming pool is 50 meters wide and 100 meters long.
   室内游泳池宽 50 米、长 100 米。

语言使用

祈使句

祈使句通常表示请求、命令、建议等，谓语动词一律用原形，句子中通常不用主语，句末用惊叹号或句号。

祈使句的结构

1. 肯定的祈使句结构

（1）be+ 形容词 / 名词。

例：Be quiet for a moment.

请安静一会儿！

（2）实义动词原形＋其他成分。

例：Take this seat.

请坐。

Do be careful.

请当心。

（3）let+ 宾语＋动词原形＋其他。

例：Let's run to the police station on the fourth street.

我们去第四大街上的警察局吧！

2. 否定句的祈使句的结构

（1）Don't+ 动词原形。

例：Don't eat in the classroom.

不要在教室里吃东西。

（2）Let's+ not+ 动词原形。

例：Let's not say anything about it.

对于这件事，咱们什么也不要说。

（3）用否定副词 never 构成，以加强否定含义。

例：Never judge a person by looks.

绝不能以貌取人。

能力训练

情境 1：

服务员帮助 Hanks 先生找到其储物柜。

要求：以小组为单位总结出服务员的英文应对语句，注意服务礼貌。

参考语句：

a. Anything I can do for you?

有什么可以为您效劳的吗？

b. If there's anything I can do to help, please let me know.
   如果需要我的帮助，您随时告诉我。

c. May I know your locker number, please?
   您的更衣室号码是多少？

d. That's at the other end of the corridor. Follow me. Please. I'll show you to your locker.
   更衣室在走廊的尽头。请跟我来，我领您去。

e. It's my pleasure to serve you. Please enjoy your stay.
   很高兴为您效劳。祝您愉快。

情境 2：

每组选出一名学生扮演 Hanks 先生，一名学生扮演健身房服务员，服务程序全面。

参考语句：

a. Are you our hotel guest, sir?
   先生，您是住店客人吗？

b. Could you please show us your room card to register?
   请您出示房卡，我们用于登记。

要求：两人一组，完成对话，注意服务礼貌。

学习任务2　Swimming and Bowling Service（泳池及保龄球服务）

工作任务	Swimming and Bowling Service（泳池及保龄球服务）	教学模式	线上线下混合教学模式 情境模拟教学模式
建议学时	4学时	教学地点	智慧教室或多媒体教室
任务描述	Hanks先生等一行七人入住沈阳丽都索菲特酒店后，对酒店提供的接待、餐饮及商务服务都非常满意。本课时针对Hanks先生一行人到酒店泳池游泳而展开英文服务对话		
学习目标	1．能够熟练地用英文表达游泳用品及泳池服务常用语。 2．能够熟练地用英文表达保龄球服务常用语。 3．掌握泳池服务及保龄球服务程序及各个程序里常用的英文语句。 4．能用英文询问客人有无其他需求，并满足客人需求。 5．培养学生解决问题的能力		

头脑风暴

1．进行泳池服务需要掌握哪些学过的基本语句？
2．需要掌握哪些泳池用品英文单词？
3．遇到紧急情况如何急救，急救用语的英文怎么说？

词汇储备

1．degree　度
2．temperature　温度
3．centigrade　摄氏度
4．swim　游泳
5．swimming pool　游泳池
6．indoor swimming pool　室内游泳池
7．outdoor swimming pool　室外游泳池
8．children's pool　儿童泳池
9．life guard　救生员
10．nurse　护士
11．bowling alley　保龄球馆
12．bowling center　保龄球中心
13．bowling　保龄球

14. lane 球道
15. turn on one's lane 打开球道
16. size 尺码

服务流程

泳池及急救服务流程如下：

1. Asking the guest if they are the guests of the hotel.
   询问客人是否是住店客人。
2. Asking the guest if they need any help.
   询问客人是否需要帮助。
3. Explaining the rules of the service.
   向客人解释服务规则。
4. Expressing the wishes.
   表达祝愿。

保龄球服务

情境模拟

1. The first step: Asking the guest if they are the guests of the hotel.
   第一步：问候客人或询问客人是否是住店客人。常用的句子有：
   a. Good morning, sir, welcome to our swimming pool.
      早上好，先生，欢迎来到我们的泳池。
   b. Good evening, ladies and gentlemen, welcome to our bowling alley.
      晚上好，女士们和先生们，欢迎来到我们的保龄球场。
   c. Good afternoon, are you the guests living in our hotel?
      下午好，您住在酒店吗？
   d. Good afternoon, have you got a member card?
      下午好，您有会员卡吗？
2. The second step: Asking the guest if they need any help.
   第二步：询问客人是否需要帮助。常用的句子有：
   a. Sir, do you need any help?
      先生，需要帮助吗？
   b. I am very pleased to provide the bowling service to you all.
      很高兴为大家提供保龄球服务。
   c. Certainly. Wait for a moment, please.
      当然可以，请稍后。
   d. How many lanes would you like to have?
      你们需要开几条球道？

e. What would you like to order?
   您想点什么？

f. I'll take the ashtray for you.
   我会把烟灰缸给您拿来。

3. The third step: Explaining the rules of the service.
   第三步：向客人解释服务规则。常用的句子有：

   a. We are open till 11 p.m.
      我们开业到晚上 11 点。

   b. Sir/Miss, excuse me, the health club will be closed in 5 minutes.
      先生/女士，健身俱乐部将在 5 分钟后关门。

   c. The bowling alley is open from 10:00 a.m. to 12:00 midnight.
      保龄球馆从上午 10 点开到午夜 12 点。

   d. The water's temperature is thirty-eight degrees centigrade.
      水温是 38 ℃。

   e. Let me show you to the locker room.
      我领您去更衣室。

   f. I'll take the ashtray for you.
      我去给您拿烟灰缸。

   g. Children under 12 are not allowed to use the pool unless accompanied by a parent.
      12 岁以下儿童必须在家长的陪同下才可以下泳池。

4. The fourth step: Expressing the wishes.
   第四步：表达祝愿。常用的句子有：

   a. (I) hope you'll have a nice day.
      祝您愉快。

   b. Please contact us if you need any help.
      如果您需要任何帮助请联系我。

   c. Thanking for coming.
      感谢光顾。

   d. Please don't hesitate to let me know if you need any help.
      如果您需要任何帮助请联系我。

   e. Look forward to seeing you again.
      期待再次见面。

能力进阶

游泳及保龄球服务过程中的特殊情况、服务程序常用的句子有：

a. Our pool is 60 meters wide and 120 meters long.
   我们的泳池 60 米宽、120 米长。

b. The temperature is 30 degrees centigrade now.
现在水温是 30 ℃。

c. According to our policies, children under 12 are not allowed to use the swimming pool unless accompanied by his/her father or mother.
我们规定，12 岁以下儿童需在父亲或母亲的陪同下才能下水。

d. Our hotel life guard and nurse are on hand.
我们的救生员和护士随时待命。

e. We change the water every day, and we just changed this morning.
我们每天都换水，今早刚换完。

f. Make sure that all your belongings are locked in the lockers.
务必确保您的物品锁在储物柜里。

g. We can't be responsible for the theft.
我们对偷窃行为不负责任。

h. I will turn the lane for you.
我为你们把球道打开。

i. What are your sizes of shoes?
你们穿几码的鞋？

j. The lanes are ready. Have a nice evening.
球道已经准备好了，祝你们夜晚时光愉快。

语言使用

祈使句的用法

1. 表示命令。如：
   Nobody move.
   任何人都不许动。

2. 表示请求。如：
   Please help me for a few minutes.
   请帮我几分钟。
   Do forgive me, I didn't mean to be rude.
   务请原谅，我无心对你粗鲁无礼。

3. 表示建议。如：
   Help yourself to a bottle of beer.
   喝瓶啤酒吧。
   Have another cup of coffee.
   再喝一杯咖啡吧。
   以 let's 开头的祈使句通常表示建议。如：
   Let's go to the cinema tonight.

今晚咱们去看电影吧。

4. 表示叮嘱。如：

Stay in bed for a couple of days.

卧床休息几天。

Look over what you've written before handing it to the examiner.

先把你写的看一遍，再交给考官。

5. 表示祝愿。如：

Have a pleasant journey.

祝您一路愉快。

6. 表示邀请。如：

Come and play a game of bridge with us.

来跟我们一起打桥牌吧。

Come and have dinner with us soon.

一会儿来跟我们一起吃饭吧。

7. 表示指引。如：

Walk to the corner, turn right and cross the road.

走到那个拐角，然后向右拐穿过马路。

能力训练

情境 1：

在泳池健身一段时间后，Hanks 先生等人要点饮品（咖啡和饮料），结合餐饮单元学习内容，完成任务要求。

要求：以小组为单位总结出服务员的英文应对语句，注意服务礼貌、禁忌。注意主要英文表达语句。

情境 2：

每组选出一名学生扮演 Hanks 先生，一名学生扮演保龄球服务中心的服务员服务程序全面。

要求：两人一组，完成对话，注意服务礼貌、禁忌。

能力拓展

康乐中心服务英语 50 句

1. Fancy going to Fitness Center tonight?

   今晚想去康乐中心吗？

2. The Fitness Center has facilities like a very big swimming pool, a gym, a billiards room and a bowling room.

   康乐中心设有一个非常大的游泳池、健身房、台球厅和保龄球房。

3. Welcome to our sauna parlor!

欢迎光临桑拿室！

4. What would you like for drinks and snacks?
   您想要点什么饮料和小吃？

5. What kind of massage is your liking?
   您喜欢哪一种按摩？

6. How many games would you like to play?
   您想玩几局？

7. Don't worry! We have full-time coaches to insure your safety.
   别担心！我们有专职教练保证您的安全。

8. Never mind! Ours are all quality products.
   不用担心！我们用的都是优质产品。

9. Take your time. I'm at your service at any time.
   别着急，慢慢来，我随时愿意为您效劳。

10. Enjoy yourself!
    尽情享受吧！

11. How would you like your hair cut, sir?
    先生，您喜欢什么发式？

12. Would you like me to trim your beard?
    要不要修一下胡子？

13. Would you like a face massage?
    要不要按摩面部？

14. What style do you want, madam?
    女士，您想要什么样式？

15. Would you like a new hair-style?
    您想换个新的发型吗？

16. Here are some pictures of hair styles.
    这里有一些发型式样的照片。

17. This style is very popular now.
    这个款式现在很流行。

18. May I invite you to this Waltz?
    我可以请您跳这支华尔兹吗？

19. Will you accept my arm?
    请您跳个舞好吗？

20. Can you oblige me with a dance?
    可以请您跳个舞吗？

21. Would you like to join me for this disco dance?
    你愿意和我一起跳迪斯科舞吗？

22. You're the best partner I've ever danced with.
    你是我经历过的最好的舞伴。
23. I'm sorry. I don't quite understand. Should I get the manager?
    很抱歉，我不是很明白。我能让经理过来吗？
24. We have a well-equipped keep-fit gym, with all the latest recreational sports apparatus: exercise bicycles, weights, wall bars and etc.
    我们体育馆有许多最先进的运动设施，像运动脚踏车、举重设备、游泳池、网球场等。
25. Could you tell me what facilities you have here?
    你能告诉我这里有什么设施吗？
26. What services do you have if I may ask?
    你能告诉我这里有什么服务吗？
27. We have a sauna bath with a massage service there, too.
    我们有桑拿浴室并提供按摩服务。
28. The kids were disappointed that the pool wasn't open this morning, though.
    今天游泳池没有开，孩子们非常失望。
29. Don't you look at yourself in the mirror too?
    难道你自己不照镜子吗？
30. They must work out all the time.
    他们一定得一直锻炼。
31. Why do you go to the gym so much?
    你为什么经常去健身房？
32. It's good for me to be healthy.
    身体健康对我有好处。
33. It's never good to put such a high value on appearances.
    如此重视外表是不好的。
34. My muscles feel numb.
    我感觉肌肉麻木。
35. I can't move a muscle.
    我一动也动不了了。
36. I'm exhausted.
    我累坏了。
37. I'm going to spend a few more minutes on the exercise bike.
    我要在骑车器上再锻炼一会儿。
38. It's too crowded in the gym at night.
    晚上健身房里太拥挤了。
39. Someone needs to fix the leg press machine.
    得有人来修理一下压腿机。

40. I'm going to relax in the sauna.
    我要去泡桑拿，放松一下。

41. How many more exercises do you have to do?
    你还要再做多少运动？

42. How often do you work out?
    你每隔多久锻炼一次？

43. So he has to exercise often. He's a firefighter.
    他是个消防队员，所以他必须经常运动。

44. I'm afraid the water is too cool to swim in.
    恐怕水太凉了，没法游泳。

45. The service hour is from 9:00 a.m. to 12:00 p.m., and we charge thirty Yuan for one game.
    我们的营业时间是从上午 9 点到午夜 12 点，我们每局收费 30 元。

46. Can I take my ten-year-old son with me to the bowling room.
    我可以带我十岁的儿子一起打保龄球吗？

47. There are four ball-lanes in our bowling room.
    我们的保龄球室有四个球道。

48. I have heard that there are dry and wet saunas.
    我听说有干式桑拿和湿式桑拿两种。

49. Massage is one of the traditional Chinese methods for building the physique.
    按摩是中国传统的强身健体的方法之一。

50. What color do you prefer for your nail-polish?
    指甲油你喜欢什么颜色的？

项目 5

The Business Center（商务中心）

学习任务 1 Booking Tickets（票务服务）

工作任务	Booking Tickets （票务服务）	教学模式	线上线下混合教学模式 情境模拟教学模式
建议学时	4学时	教学地点	智慧教室或多媒体教室
任务描述	Hanks先生等一行七人入住沈阳丽都索菲特酒店几天后，今天Hanks先生来到商务中心要求订票。商务中心订票人员的工作任务有哪些？		
学习目标	1. 能够熟练地用英文订购机票等服务的常用语。 2. 能够用英文询问客人的服务需求，并满足客人的需求。 3. 能准确填写客人所需交通工具、抵离时间和地点等信息，并与客人进行确认。 4. 能够准确无误地用英文介绍可以提供的服务项目。 5. 掌握订票服务的服务程序及各个程序里常用的英文语句。 6. 熟悉服务外宾应有的礼仪和禁忌。 7. 培养学生解决问题的能力		

项目 5　The Business Center（商务中心）

头脑风暴

1. 酒店的订票服务需要哪些常用语言？用英文怎么说？
2. 如果你是酒店商务中心订票工作人员，服务程序是什么？各个程序应如何与客人进行英语沟通？
3. 如果客人对服务不满意，怎么用英语与客人沟通？

词汇储备

商务中心票务服务主要项目及有关术语：

transportation route　交通路线图
air-ticket booking　机票预订
train ticket booking office　火车票预订处
flight　航班
airport　机场
economic class　经济舱
business class　商务舱
train station　火车站
train number　车次
soft-sleeping berth　软卧
express train　快车
ordinary train　普快
slow train　慢车

服务流程

订票服务流程如下：

1. Asking for the requirements of the guest.
   询问客人需求。
2. Recording the guest's demand accurately and making a confirmation.
   准确记录客人需求并做核对。
3. Asking the guest to show his certificates or other identification materials.
   让客人出示证件或其他身份证明材料。
4. Expressing the wishes.
   表达祝愿。

预订火车票服务

情境模拟

1. The first step: Asking for the requirements of the guest.
   第一步：询问客人需求。常用的句子有：

153

a. which day's tickets would you like?
   您想预订哪天的票？
b. First class or economy class?
   头等舱还是经济舱？
c. Which train would you like to take?
   您想乘坐哪次火车？

2. The second step: Recording the guest's demand accurately and making a confirmation.
   第二步：准确记录客人需求并做核对。常用的句子有：

   a. There is a flight of the International Airline at 10:20 a.m., is that all right?
      上午有10点20有一次国际航班，对吗？
   b. I'm afraid it's not very easy to book the ticket, because now the traffic is very heavy for the spring transportation, the tickets are in great demand.
      恐怕很难订票，因为现在是春季运输高峰期，（飞机、火车）票的需求量很大。

3. The third step: Asking the guest to show his certificates or other identification materials.
   第三步：让客人出示证件或其他身份证明材料。常用的句子有：

   a. May I have you passport, please?
      请您出示护照，可以吗？
   b. Could you please show me you Identification Card in order to make a registration?
      请您出示身份证用于登记，可以吗？

4. The fourth step: Expressing the wishes.
   第四步：表达祝愿。常用的句子有：

   a. (I) Hope you'll have a nice day.
      祝您愉快。
   b. Please contact us if you need any help.
      如果您需要任何帮助，请联系我。
   c. We look forward to another chance to serve you, sir.
      先生，我期待下次为您服务。

能力进阶

如因特殊原因导致交通高峰，票源紧张不能满足客人需求时，与客人沟通的技巧有：

a. There are two flights: one is 8 o'clock in the morning, the other is 5 o'clock in the afternoon.
   有两次航班，一个是上午8点，另一个是下午5点。
b. First class or economy class?
   头等舱还是经济舱？
c. And a window seat or an aisle seat?
   靠窗的座位还是过道？

d. Let me have a check. There are two trains leaving for Chongqing on that day, one is express, and the other is ordinary. What kind of trains do you prefer?

我核对一下。当天有两次火车去重庆，一个是高铁，另一个是普快。您更喜欢哪个？

e. Mr. Smith, the booking office said that all tickets for hard sleeping berth had been sold out. Now they have only tickets for hard seat, do you like to buy?

Smith 先生，预订处说所有的卧铺票都已售空。现在只有硬座票，您还买吗？

语言使用

can /could you...?

can 表示能力时，译为"能""会""可以"。过去式为 could，表达过去能力的概念。否定式则是在其后直接加上 not，变为 cannot/can not，缩略为 can't。同理，过去式的否定式为 could not，缩略为 couldn't。

can /could you...? 请求别人为你做某事的一种表达法。意思是"你能不能（可不可以）为我或帮我做……"

e.g.: Could you please show me your ID card?

请您出示身份证。

Could you please tell me your cell phone number?

您能告诉我您的手机号码吗？

能力训练

情境 1：

王先生来到商务中心要求订购去北京的机票。要求经济舱并靠近窗户的座位。

要求：以小组为单位总结出票务人员的英文应对语句，注意服务礼貌、禁忌。

情境 2：

1 月 22 日，酒店客人 Smith 先生到商务中心要求订一张 2 月 1 日"北京—重庆"的火车硬卧票。由于恰逢春运高峰，可能火车票比较紧张。播放一段有关情境的音频，学生们从音频中总结出相应的英文语句。

要求：以小组为单位总结出服务员的英文应对语句，注意服务礼貌、禁忌。

学习任务 2　Secretarial Service（文秘服务）

工作任务	Secretarial Service（文秘服务）	教学模式	线上线下混合教学模式 情境模拟教学模式
建议学时	4 学时	教学地点	智慧教室或多媒体教室
任务描述	Hanks 先生等一行七人入住沈阳丽都索菲特酒店后，今天要在会议室召开会议。Hanks 先生到商务中心要求复印会议资料		
学习目标	1．能够熟练地用英文表达复印、打字等服务的常用语。 2．能够用英文询问客人的服务需求，并将客人的需求准确记录下来并予以确认。 3．能用英文回答客人问询并解释有关事项，说明资费标准，并弄清付款方式。 4．培养学生分析问题及解决问题的能力		

头脑风暴

1．酒店的文件处理需要哪些设施？用英文怎么说？

2．如果你是酒店商务中心工作人员，文件处理的服务程序是什么？各个程序应如何与客人进行英语沟通？

3．如果客人对收费等服务不满意，怎么用英语与客人沟通？

词汇储备

文件处理设施

folder　文件夹
format　格式化
laminate　压膜
magic marker　荧光笔
paper clip　回形针
safety pin　安全别针
staple remover　起钉器
stapler　订书机
printer　复印机

服务流程

服务流程如下：

1．Asking for the requirements of the guest.
　　询问客人的需求。

项目 5　The Business Center（商务中心）

2. Recording the guest's demand accurately and making confirmation.
   准确记录客人的需求并做核实。

3. Explaining the service charge and the way of payment.
   解释服务费及支付方式。

4. Expressing the wishes.
   表达祝愿。

情境模拟

1. Copying.
   复印。

   a. I'd like to copy this.
      我想要复印这个文件。

   b. How many copies would you like?
      您想要复印多少份？

会议服务　　收发传真服务

   c. Would you like me to make it a little darker/lighter?
      我给您的复印件打暗些还是亮些？

   d. Would you like me to staple these for you?
      给您装订起来吗？

   e. Shall I copy these on both sides to the paper?
      这些文件需要双面打印吗？

   f. Your original is not very clear. I can't guarantee the copy will be good.
      您的原文不太清楚。我不能保证复印件是好的。

2. Sending a fax.
   发传真。

   a. To New York it's 10 yuan per minute, including/excluding service charge.
      到纽约每分钟10元，包括/不包括服务费。

   b. The minimum charge is 15 yuan.
      最低收费是15元。

   c. Please write down the country code, the area code and their number.
      请写下国家代码、区号和他们的号码。

   d. Shall I make a copy of this, and then send the copy?
      复印一份，然后寄出去吗？

3. Typing.
   打字。

   a. What font and size would you like?
      您想要什么字体和字号？

   b. Shall I make the space larger?

我要把空白扩大一点吗？

c．Could you check it?

您能检查一下吗？

4．Expressing the wishes.

表达祝愿。

a．(I) hope you'll have a nice day.

祝您今天愉快。

b．Please contact us if you need any help.

如果您需要任何帮助请联系我。

c．Please don't hesitate to let me know if you need any help.

如果您需要任何帮助请联系我。

能力进阶

文秘服务过程中的特殊情况、服务程序常用的句子有：

情境1：Hanks 先生来到商务中心想打印一份文件资料，得知打印收费标准为每张 8 元人民币后，Hanks 先生与工作人员商量能不能优惠一些。

a．The charge is 8 RMB per page.

每张收费8元。

b．That's too expensive. Can I have it cheaper?

太贵了，能便宜些吗？

c．Sorry. It's said by the hotel regulation. However, you can ask the Lobby Assistant Manager for a discount.

抱歉，这是酒店规定。不过，您可以问一下大堂助理是否有折扣。

情境2：Hanks 先生来到商务中心打印材料，就复印的细节与他进行对话，如纸张大小、字体颜色、如何付款等。

a．What size would you like o have for the copies?

您想复印多大尺寸？

b．What color would you like color or colorless?

您想复印彩色还是黑白的？

c．Please have a look, is the color of this testing-paper good enough?

请看，复印纸颜色如何？

e．Pay in cash or go with your room charge?

您是付现金还是记入房账？

语言使用

may I...? 用法

may I...? 是比较委婉的询问别人允许的句型，might 的语气更加委婉。

e.g.: May I come round in the morning?
我早上来可以吗？
May I have your room number?
您的房间号是多少？

能力训练

情境 1：
Hanks 先生来到商务中心，要求小李帮忙打印一份文件资料，打印收费标准为每张 12 元人民币，Hanks 先生与工作人员就价格进行沟通。

要求：以小组为单位总结出服务员的英文应对语句，注意服务礼仪。

情境 2：
Hanks 先生到商务中心打印材料，碰到机器出故障了，修理工今晚会来修理，工作人员应该如何处理。

要求：以小组为单位总结出服务员的英文应对语句，注意服务礼仪。

能力拓展

商务中心服务英语 90 句

1. I'd like to have these copied.
   我想复印这些资料。

2. What time do you expect it?
   您什么时候要？

3. I'll send it to your room as soon as I finish typing.
   我一打完就送到您房间去。

4. How many copies would you like?
   您需要复印多少份？

5. Would you like me to make it a little darker/lighter?
   要不要我（把颜色）调深/浅一些？

6. I'll leave the original here. Please call me when the copy is ready.
   我把原件放在这里，等复印好了就打电话通知我吧。

7. Would you like me to staple these for you?
   我为您装订好这些，好吗？

8. Shall I staple them on the left side or at the top?
   我是装订在左侧还是上边呢？

9. Shall I enlarge / reduce this to fit A4 paper?
   我是不是把它放大/缩小到合适 A4 纸张的大小呢？

10. Shall I copy these on both sides to the paper?
    我进行双面复印，好吗？

11. We don't have paper that large. Shall we copy it to two pieces, and then tape them together?

    我们没有这么大的纸。我们分开两块复印，然后再粘在一起，好吗？

12. It is out of ink.

    没墨了。

13. Your original is not very clear. I can't guarantee the copy will be good.

    您的原件不太清晰，我不能保证复印件的效果很好。

14. The machine is out of order.

    机器出故障了。

15. A repairman is coming to fix it this evening.

    修理工今晚会来修理。

16. I'll call you as soon as the machine is fixed.

    机器一修好，我就给您打电话。

17. I'd like to send a fax.

    我想要发份传真。

18. To... it's 10 yuan per minute, including / excluding service charge.

    发传真到……是每分钟 10 元，包括 / 不包括服务费。

19. The minimum charge is 15 Yuan.

    最低收费是 15 元。

20. Please write down the country code, the area code and their number.

    请写下国家代号、区号和他们的号码。

21. The paper is too trick / thin. It may jam the machine.

    这张纸太厚 / 薄，可能会卡纸的。

22. Shall I make a copy of this, and then send the copy?

    我复印一份，然后将复印件传真过去，好吗？

23. Mr.... this is... from the Business Center. We have received a fax for you.

    ……先生，我是商务中心的……我们收到给您的一份传真。

24. What font and size would you like?

    您想要什么字体，多大号的？

25. What size would you like to have for the copies?

    请问您要使用多大的纸张？

26. What color would you like, Color or colorless?

    请问是用彩色的还是黑白的？

27. Shall I make the space larger?

    我把行距拉开一些好吗？

28. The title is Arial and the text is Times New Roman.

    标题用 Arial 体，正文用 Times New Roman 体。

29. When do I send the first draft to you for proofreading after I finish typing?
    我把初稿打印好后，什么时候送给您校对比较合适？

30. Could you check it?
    您检查一下，好吗？

31. Please indent the first line of each paragraph.
    请把每个段落的首行缩进一些。

32. Shall I save it on your disk?
    我把它存在您的磁盘上，好吗？

33. I'm afraid we can only save it on our disks, in case of any virus.
    恐怕我们只能存在我们的磁盘上，以防有病毒。

34. Excuse me, how can I get to the Guangzhou International Conference and Exhibition Center?
    打扰了，我怎么去广州国际会展中心？

35. The public phone is beside the elevator.
    公用电话在电梯旁边。

36. Could you give me some information about the transportation?
    你能为我提供交通方面的情况吗？

37. You may take Bus No.37.
    您可以乘 37 路公共汽车去。

38. If you take a taxi, it will take you 15 minutes.
    如果您搭的士去的话，大概要 15 分钟。

39. It may cost you 20 to 25 Yuan.
    花费大概是 20 至 25 元。

40. You may go there by train. Here is the timetable.
    您可以乘火车去。这儿有时刻表。

41. There are several flights a day.
    每天有几次航班。

42. We can book a ticket for you.
    我们可以为您订票。

43. I'd like to post a letter.
    我要寄一封信。

44. I'd like to send a parcel.
    我要寄一个包裹。

45. How much is the postage?
    邮费是多少？

46. I can't say for sure now.
    我现在还不清楚。

47. I'll let you know later, will that be all right?
    我迟一些告诉您，可以吗？

48. We're going to have a congress next Monday. I'd like to book some facilities and personnel for it.
    我们下星期一要举行一个会议，我来预订一些必要的设备和人员。

49. Yes. We need an auditorium for 40 people, a projector and a video-camera.
    对。我们要一间能容纳 40 人的礼堂、一个投影机和一部摄像机。

50. Everything will be ready Friday afternoon. Could you come and check it?
    这个星期五下午一切就能准备就绪。您到时来检查一下，好吗？

51. We're going to have a two-day congress here next week.
    我们下周要开一个为期两天的会议。

52. We'd like to book some facilities and personnel for it.
    我们要预订一些设施和人员。

53. We need a simultaneous interpreter for Monday, and a consecutive interpreter for Tuesday.
    我们周一需要一名同声传译，周二需要一名接续传译。

54. Do you need any messenger boys?
    你们需要勤务员吗？

55. Your signature and telephone number here, please.
    请您在这里签字，并且留下电话号码。

56. Everything will be ready by Saturday afternoon.
    周六下午我们会准备好一切的。

57. If there is anything I can do, please let me know.
    如果有什么我能为您效劳的，请告诉我。

58. Is there any flight to Beijing on July, 4th?
    7 月 4 日有飞往北京的班机吗？

59. May I have your passport, please?
    能把您的护照给我吗？

60. First class or economy class?
    头等舱还是经济舱？

61. Is there a non-stop flight to London?
    有直达伦敦的航班吗？

62. I would like a non-smoking seat.
    我想要非吸烟区的座位。

63. I'd like to reserve a sleeper to Chicago.
    我要预订去芝加哥的卧铺。

64. Which day's tickets would you like?

项目 5　The Business Center（商务中心）

您要哪一天的票？

65. Which seats would you like?

您要什么位子？

66. First seats would you like?

您要头等舱还是经济舱？

67. Which train would you like to take?

您想坐哪次车？

68. Do you have any tickets left for... show?

还有……演出的票吗？

69. One way or a round trip ticket?

单程票还是双程票？

70. Where do I pick up the ticket?

我到什么地方拿机票？

71. I'm afraid that flight/train/show is fully booked.

恐怕那个航班／火车／演出的票已经订完了。

72. There are no seats available on the flight leaving at 16: 15.

在 16 点 15 分起飞的航班，座位票已售完。

73. How about a soft berth ticket?

软卧怎么样？

74. How long is the ticket valid?

这张车票的有效期是多久？

75. This is the Business Center. I'm Li, an employee here. What can I do for you?

这里是商务中心，我是这里的工作人员，姓李，请问有什么可以帮忙的吗？

76. The charge is RMB 1.2 Yuan per page, the total is RMB 48 Yuan. What way would you like to pay? Pay in cash or go with your room charge?

我们的收费标准是每张 1.2 元人民币，费用一共是 48 元人民币。请问您如何付账呢？是记入房账还是直接付现金？

77. The charge is RMB 8 Yuan per page.

我们按每张 8 元人民币收费。

78. I'd like to ask you to arrange a Spanish interpreter for me.

我想请你帮我联系一位会讲西班牙语的翻译。

79. The interpreter must know well about the terminology in the art of architecture and have trade-talk experiences.

这位翻译必须精通建筑学方面的专业术语，拥有商务洽谈经验。

80. The interpreter had better come to see me no later than this afternoon for a communication in advance.

翻译人员最好能今天下午到位，以便我们提前沟通一下。

163

81. May I know your way of payment?

    请问您的付款方式？

82. Please count into my room charge directly.

    直接记入房账吧。

83. I'll contact with the Translation Company at once and inform you as soon as possible after the interpreter is chosen.

    我马上与翻译公司取得联系，找好翻译人员后，便立即通知您。

84. Please sit down here, give me the manuscripts.

    您先请坐，把原稿给我吧。

85. The fax machine is on work, please tell me the number.

    传真机已准备好，请告诉我对方的传真号码。

86. Mr. Smith, the receiver has got all pages of the fax, this is your manuscript, please keep it well.

    Smith 先生，传真已经发过去了，对方已确认全部收悉。这是您的原稿，请收好。

87. If you have anything for help, please contact with me.

    如果您还有事情需要帮忙，请与我联系。

88. We have just received a fax for Mr. Smith in room 1105. Could you please send it to his room at once?

    我们刚收到一份给 1105 号房 Smith 先生的传真，请你尽快将这份传真送到他的房间，好吗？

89. Please sign on the form; give me a reply after it has been sent to Mr. Smith's room.

    请你签收一下，交给 Smith 先生后请回复我们确认一下。

90. The Internet charge in 30 minutes is 10 Yuan.

    半个小时的上网收费 10 元。

任务工单

项目 1　The Front Office（前厅部）

学习任务 1　Room Reservation（客房预订服务）

任务工单 1　理论测试

1. 词组互译

（1）客房预订（n.）_____　　（2）标准间_____

（3）家庭套房_____　　　　 （4）房型_____

（5）双人间（配大床）_____　（6）date of birth _____

（7）reservation record _____（8）room availability _____

（9）peak season _____　　　（10）waiting list _____

2. 单项选择

（1）Which date would that _____ ?

　　A. being　　　　B. are　　　　C. is　　　　D. be

（2）What does "American Express" mean?

　　A. credit card　　B. mail　　　C. country　　D. person's name

（3）We are looking forward to _____ you.

　　A. serve　　　　B. service　　C. serving　　D. served

（4）The guests can usually pay their hotel bills by all the ways below, except _____.

　　A. by credit card　B. by Visa card　C. by cash　D. by mail

（5）The word "reserve" equals to _____ in hotel field.

　　A. serve　　　　B. book　　　C. invest　　D. settle the bill

（6）A: _____? B: Yes, I'd like to book a room for my friend, Cray Smith.

　　A. How are you　B. May I help you　C. Hello　D. How do you do

（7）Do you need _____ service, sir?

　　A. pick-on　　　B. pick-of　　C. pick-up　　D. pick-off

（8）Sorry, we are _____ booked in the period.

　　A. fully　　　　B. full　　　　C. fulling　　D. fulled

（9）Among all the room types, which one is the most expensive? _____.

　　A. Triple room　B. Business suite　C. Deluxe suite　D. Presidential suite

（10）A: I'd like to make an adjustment of my reservation.

　　B: Certainly, sir. May I have the date of your _____, please?

A．reservation　　B．departure　　C．flight　　D．train

3．多项选择

（1）A: I'd like to reserve a room at your hotel?

B: _____ , please.

A．Hold on　　B．Hold the line　　C．Hold up　　D．Hold

（2）A: What _____ of room would you like?

B: I'd like a single room.

A．type　　B．rate　　C．size　　D．kind

（3）What's the difference between guaranteed reservation and unguaranteed reservation? _____

A．For guaranteed reservation, the hotel will hold the room overnight for the guest.

B．For unguaranteed reservation, the hotel will hold the room by sometime the same day.

C．For guaranteed reservation, the hotel will hold the room by sometime the same day.

D．For unguaranteed reservation, the hotel will hold the room overnight for the guest.

（4）As a reservationist, when we want to know the guest name, what should we ask? _____

A．May I have your name, please?　　B．May I know your name, please?

C．What's your name?　　D．Tell me your name.

（5）Choose the right ones: "我将为您取消您的预订". _____

A．I will cancel your reservation.　　B．I will call off your reservation.

C．I will extend your reservation.　　D．I will change your reservation.

（6）Choose the right ones: "很抱歉让您久等了". _____

A．Sorry to have kept you waiting.　　B．I'm sorry to have kept you waiting.

C．Sorry to keep you waiting.　　D．I'm Sorry to keep you waiting.

（7）A: _____ fill in the registration form?

B: OK.

A．Would you mind　　B．Would you please

C．Please　　D．Would you like to

（8）The guest can make the payment by the following ways _____.

A．in cash　　B．with traveler's check

C．by credit card　　D．by mail

（9）Choose the right ones: "标准间每晚 498 元." _____

A．The standard room costs 498 Yuan per night.

B．The standard room is 498 Yuan per night.

C．498 Yuan per night for a standard room.

D．498 Yuan a night on a standard room

（10）Choose the right ones: "请问您住多久？" _____

A．How long will you be staying?　　B．How long will you stay?

C．How much will you be staying?　　D．How much will you stay?

167

任务工单 2　技能操作

工作任务	Room Reservation（客房预订服务）					
姓名		班级		学号		日期
情境演练	根据情境词提示，两人一组完成对话（情境二选一） A：提示词：arrival date, double room, 3 nights, quiet, 388 Yuan B：提示词：cancel, meeting, double room, standard room 每组每个角色不得少于 6 句，在同学面前展示，学生互评，教师点评					
技能演练	下面是一封来自外国客人的订房邮件，读一读，并用英文写一封回复件 Dear Sir or Madam, 　　I'd like to reserve a family suite for my parents and my son, from October 14th to 21th, if possible, with a balcony and facing the south. We require twin beds. 　　Please let me know the daily rate including breakfast. 　　Yours sincerely, 　　Lucy Green					
评估	 教师签字：					
自我反思	 学生签字：					

学习任务 2　Check In（入住登记服务）

任务工单 1　理论测试

1．词组互译

（1）入住登记_____　　　　（2）前台_____

（3）团队客人_____　　　　（4）填写_____

（5）护照号码_____　　　（6）预订记录_____

（7）酒店大厅_____　　　（8）房号_____

（9）房卡_____　　　（10）微信付款_____

（11）walk in guest _____　　　（12）make the payment _____

（13）breakfast coupon _____　　　（14）TWB _____

（15）presidential suite _____　　　（16）20 percent _____

（17）standard room _____　　　（18）registration form _____

（19）scan the QR code _____　　　（20）group leader _____

2. 根据句意填空（每空一词）

R=Receptionist（接待员）　G=Guest（客人）

（1）R: Good morning. Is _____ anything else I can do _____ you?

G: I'd like to check in.

（2）R: _____ I _____ your passport?

G: Certainly, here you are.

（3）G: I'd like to extend my reservation. _____

R: OK. In _____ name was the reservation made?

（4）R: _____ would you like to _____?

G: In cash.

（5）R: Good afternoon, welcome to our hotel, _____ is your group leader?

G: Good afternoon. I'm the group leader.

（6）G: What's the _____ _____ per night?

R: It's 680 Yuan RMB per night.

（7）R: Would you mind _____ _____ this registration form?

G: Sure, give me a pen please.

（8）R: Your room is 809, it is _____ the 8th floor.

G: OK, I see.

（9）R: Please _____ at the bottom on the right hand side?

G: Sure.

（10）R: The bellboy will _____ your luggage and _____ you up to your room.

G: Thank you so much for your help.

3. 翻译句子

（1）不用谢，我很高兴随时为您服务。

（2）门童会带领您到您的房间，祝您入住愉快。

（3）请填写入住登记表。

（4）对不起，让您久等了。

（5）White 小姐，您订了四个晚上的一个标准间和一个商务套房，对吗？

（6）How would you like to settle your bill?

（7）Do you have a reservation with our hotel?

（8）Here is your receipt and please keep it.

（9）Please sign at the bottom of the right hand side.

（10）Your room is 505 and is on the 5th floor.

任务工单 2　技能操作

工作任务	Check In（入住登记服务）					
姓名		班级		学号		日期
情境演练	类型：入住登记 客人：Tom Smith, a tour leader（领队） 预订信息：20 TWBs for 20 persons；2 nights 入住登记：（需更改成）22 TWBs for 23 persons；2 nights 特殊需求：special rate（最终给了 15% 的折扣）					
评估	 教师签字：					
自我反思	 学生签字：					

学习任务 3　Exchanging Foreign Currency（外币兑换服务）

任务工单 1　理论测试

1. 词组互译

（1）填写 _____　　　（2）给您 _____
（3）免费早餐 _____　　（4）服务费 _____
（5）把……退换成…… _____　（6）foreign currency _____
（7）HongKong dollar _____　（8）according to _____
（9）Euro _____　　　　（10）exchange memo _____

2. 单项选择

（1）A: What kind of room would you like, sir?

　　B: _____.

　　A．Double room, please.　　B．Yes, I would
　　C．No, I would not　　　　　D．Yes, please

（2）The word "facilities" means _____.

　　A．工厂　　B．家庭　　C．设施　　D．机械装置

（3）The word "discount" means _____.

　　A．折扣　　B．定金　　C．保险柜　　D．讨价还价

（4）The word "deposit" means _____.

　　A．预订　　B．折扣　　C．接待　　D．押金

（5）Mr. Brown wants to book a _____ room in the hotel.

　　A．two　　B．twin　　C．twice　　D．third

（6）I am sorry _____ hear that.

　　A．in　　B．on　　C．to　　D．of

（7）What's your opinion of our _____.

　　A．service　　B．serve　　C．serving　　D．serves

（8）There is a _____ Cafe on the first floor.

　　A．24 hours　　B．24-hours　　C．24-hour　　D．24 hour

（9）We don't accept tips, but thank you very much _____.

　　A．anyway　　B．anyone　　C．anywhere　　D．anyhow

（10）What does "Cashier Desk" mean in the hotel? _____.

　　A．收银台　　B．现金　　C．问讯处　　D．失物招领处

任务工单 2　技能操作

工作任务	Exchanging Foreign Currency（外币兑换服务）					
姓名		班级		学号		日期
情境演练	学生自编情境，2～3人一组完成英文外币兑换服务。 要求：角色扮演，服务程序全面，要有特殊情况处理，每组每个角色不得少于6句，在同学面前展示，学生互评，教师点评					
评估						教师签字：
自我反思						学生签字：

学习任务 4　Check Out（结账退宿服务）

任务工单 1　理论测试

1. 补全对话

C: Cashier（收银员）　G: Guest（客人）

C: Good morning. Is there anything I can do for you?

G: I want to _____ some foreign currency for souvenirs.

C: What kind of foreign currency would you like to change?

G: US dollars.

C: According to today's _____ of exchange, every US $100 in cash _____ _____ 680 Yuan. How much would you like to change, sir?

G: $400. Here you are.

C: $400. The exchange is 2 720 yuan. May I see your passport?

G: Sure. Here you are.

C: Please _____ _____ the exchange memo. Be careful to fill in your passport number, the total amount, your room number or permanent address, and _____ your name here as well.

G: Here you are. Is that all right?

C: Here is 2 720 Yuan. Please count it. Here's your memo. Please _____ onto it.

G: By the way, _____ can I change my remaining RMB back into US dollars when I go back to my country?

C: You can change it back into US dollars in the specialized foreign exchange bank or the Airport Exchange Office, and you're required to _____ the memo there, too.

G: Thanks for your help.

C: You're welcome. Glad to have served you.

2. 翻译句子

（1）你好，我想结账。

（2）White 小姐，请稍等，我帮您结算账单。您的消费金额为 6 500 美元。请您查看一下。

（3）您已预交 1 000 美元，请把收据给我。

（4）收什么信用卡？

（5）欢迎您用旅行支票付账。

3. 用英语向客人说明以下问题

（1）询问客人是付现金还是用旅行支票结账。

（2）告知客人账单为 4 567 元。

（3）向客人道别。

任务工单 2　技能操作

工作任务	Check Out（结账退宿服务）						
姓名		班级		学号		日期	
情境演练	学生自编情境，2～3人一组完成英文结账退宿服务。 要求：角色扮演，服务程序全面，要有特殊情况处理，每组每个角色不得少于6句，在同学面前展示，学生互评，教师点评						
评估	 教师签字：						
自我反思	 学生签字：						

173

项目 2　The Housekeeping（客房部）

学习任务 1　Introducing Facilities（介绍酒店设施与服务）

任务工单 1　理论测试

1. 词组互译

（1）停车场 _____　　　（2）健身中心 _____

（3）房卡 _____　　　　（4）休闲设施 _____

（5）商务中心 _____　　（6）保险箱 _____

（7）礼品店 _____　　　（8）游泳池 _____

（9）期待 _____　　　　（10）漂亮风景 _____

（11）take the lift _____　　（12）Concierge Desk _____

（13）buffet breakfast _____　（14）bowling alley _____

（15）beauty salon _____　　（16）internet access _____

（17）remote control _____　（18）conference facilities _____

（19）air conditioner _____　（20）luggage rack _____

2. 根据句意填空（每空一词）

　　R=Reservationist（预订员）　　G=Guest（客人）

（1）R: The bellboy will _____ your luggage _____ your room.

　　G: Thank you.

（2）R: Would you tell me your _____ _____, please?

　　G: It's Room 1104.

（3）G: Where is the Chinese restaurant?

　　R: It is _____ the second floor.

（4）R: Is this your first time here?

　　G: Yes, very first. _____ the _____, do you have a bar?

（5）G: How to use the air conditioner?

　　R: You can _____ the control to _____ the temperature as you like.

（6）G: Is _____ a coffee shop in your hotel?

　　R: Yes. It's on the first floor.

（7）R: Excuse me, sir. So you have 4 pieces of _____ altogether?

　　G: Yes.

(8) R: Where could I _____ your luggage?

　　G: Oh, Just leave it here.

(9) R: What _____ of car do you want to rent, sir?

　　G: A red sport car.

(10) R: Sir, _____ _____ pieces do you have?

　　G: 2 suitcases and a handbag.

任务工单 2　技能操作

工作任务	Introducing Facilities（介绍酒店设施与服务）						
姓名		班级		学号		日期	
情境演练	根据情境词提示，两人一组完成对话（情境二选一）。 行李员为客人介绍房间设施。 1. 关于调试空调温度。 2. 关于收看电视节目。 3. 关于使用室内保险箱。 4. 关于使用门把手菜单。 要求：两名同学一组，完成对话。可以选择其中的两点编写，也可以四点都编写。在同学面前展示，学生互评，教师点评						
评估	 教师签字：						
自我反思	 学生签字：						

学习任务 2　Room Cleaning Service（客房清扫服务）

任务工单 1　理论测试

1. 词组互译

(1) 台灯 _____　　　　(2) 床单 _____

(3) 茶几 _____　　　　(4) 故障房 _____

(5) 加床（v.） _____　　(6) maintenance service _____

(7) sewing kit _____　　(8) laundry list _____

(9) room attendant _____　(10) service charge _____

175

2．单项选择

（1）All the words below are used in Laundry Service except _____.

　　A．shrink　　　　B．mend　　　　C．beverage　　　　D．stain

（2）I've just taken a bath and it is quite a _____ now.

　　A．clean　　　　B．mess　　　　C．dirty　　　　D．wet

（3）We should certainly pay for the damage, but the indemnity will not _____ 10 times of the laundry charge.

　　A．exceed　　　　B．extend　　　　C．extra　　　　D．excuse

（4）It's getting dark. Would you like me to _____ the curtains for you, sir?

　　A．put　　　　B．pull　　　　C．push　　　　D．draw

（5）I'd like to know something about your _____ service.

　　A．cleaning　　　　B．laundry　　　　C．wash　　　　D．dry cleaning

（6）Sorry to disturb you, but may I _____ your room now?

　　A．do　　　　B．did　　　　C．done　　　　D．does

（7）_____ the way, how long will it take to clean the room?

　　A．With　　　　B．On　　　　C．By　　　　D．In

（8）Can you _____ the air conditioner for me?

　　A．draw　　　　B．turn in　　　　C．turn off　　　　D．make up

（9）Sorry to have _____ up your time.

　　A．take　　　　B．took　　　　C．taken　　　　D．takes

（10）A: Anything else I can do for you, sir?

　　　B: _____.

　　A．Yes, you do　　　　　　　　　　B．No, you don not

　　C．Yes, you can　　　　　　　　　　D．No, thanks for your help

3．多项选择

（1）Chambermaid: _____, may I clean your room now?

　　　Guest: Sure.

　　A．Sorry to disturb you　　　　　　B．Sorry to interrupt you

　　C．I'm sorry to disturb you　　　　D．I'm sorry to interrupt you

（2）Choose the right ones: "您什么时候方便？" _____

　　A．When would it be convenient for you?　　B．When would it be better for you?

　　C．When would me like?　　　　　　　　　D．What time would it be convenient?

（3）It's getting dark. Please help me _____.

　　A．turn off the lights　　　　　　　B．draw the curtains

　　C．turn on the lights　　　　　　　D．take away the bed cover

（4）Which of the following is not provided by Housekeeping Department? _____.

　　A．Room-Cleaning　　B．Laundry　　C．Room Reservation　　D．Luggage

（5）客房清扫服务中，"我现在可以为您打扫房间吗？"如何表达？_____

  A．May I do your room now?   B．May I clean your room now?

  C．May I make up your room now?   D．May I do up your room now?

4．根据句意填空（每空一词）

（1）我能为您做些什么吗？

  Is there _____ I can do _____ you?

（2）晚安，祝您做个好梦！

  Good _____. _____ a nice dream!

（3）先生，要我等会儿再来吗？

  Shall I _____ _____ later, sir?

（4）客房清扫服务，我可以进来吗？

  Housekeeping, may I _____ _____?

（5）如果您需要帮助，请拨打926到客房中心。

  If you need any _____, please dial 926 to the housekeeping _____.

任务工单2 技能操作

工作任务	Room Cleaning Service（客房清扫服务）			
姓名		班级	学号	日期
情境演练	服务员来到Hanks先生的房间，正准备打扫时，突然发现Hanks先生不舒服。在客人住店期间，如果发生了意外情况，应该小心沉着处理。 参考语句： a. 我为您叫医生来，好吗？ Shall I call a doctor for you? b. 在医生到来之前，我可以为您做些什么？ Anything I can do before the doctor arrives? c. 别担心。 Don't worry. d. 医生来了就好了。 The doctor is coming. e. 您很快就会好起来的。 You'll be alright soon. f. 客人得到救治以后，可以慰问一下："您觉得好些了吗？" Are you feeling better now? 要求： 1. 两人一组完成脚本的编写。 2. 表演对话。 3. 注意服务礼貌、禁忌。			
评估	教师签字：			
自我反思	学生签字：			

学习任务 3 Laundry Service（洗衣服务）

任务工单 1 理论测试

1. 词组互译

（1）洗衣单_____　　　　（2）洗衣袋_____
（3）洗衣费用1_____　　　（4）洗衣费用2_____
（5）服务费_____　　　　（6）快洗服务_____
（7）去除污点（v.）_____　（8）干洗_____
（9）不能手洗_____　　　（10）缝（扣）_____
（11）regular service _____　（12）leather jacket _____
（13）special equipment _____（14）price list _____
（15）starch and shrink _____（16）cancel the reservation _____
（17）right-hand desk drawer _____（18）silk dress _____
（19）room attendant _____（20）dyeing and mending _____

2. 根据句意填空（每空一词）

H=Housekeeping clerk（客房服务员）　　G=Guest（客人）

（1）H: For clothes _____ before 11.00 a.m., we will deliver them to your room by 9.00 p.m. the same day.

　　G: I see, thank you.

（2）H: _____ _____ does it take for dry-cleaning?

　　G: It usually takes two days.

（3）G: What if it is for press only?

　　H: It depends _____ what it is.

（4）R: _____ _____ nights will you need the room?

　　G: Two nights.

（5）H: Housekeeping, do you _____ some laundry?

　　G: No, I haven't.

（6）H: Sir, is the laundry in the laundry _____?

　　R: Yes, it is.

（7）H: _____ there anything _____ I can do for you?

　　G: No, thank you.

（8）H: Please _____ to the laundry list for further information.

　　G: Oh, I know.

（9）G: When can I get my laundry back?

　　H: We will _____ them back to you around 4 p.m. tomorrow.

（10）G: I have a clothes that needs mending. Do you have mending _____?

　　R: Yes, we have, sir.

3．单项选择

（1）Laundry bag equals to _____ in laundry service.

　　A．handbag　　　B．schoolbag　　　C．big bag　　　D．plastic bag

（2）For clothes _____ before 11 a.m., we will deliver them to you by 9 p.m.

　　A．received　　　B．receive　　　C．receives　　　D．receiving

（3）We have different _____, such as washing, dry-cleaning, ironing and mending.

　　A．service　　　B．serving　　　C．services　　　D．serves

（4）_____ does your laundry service usually take?

　　A．How much　　　B．How many　　　C．How long　　　D．How often

（5）If you are _____, we have a 2-hour express service.

　　A．in hurry　　　B．in a hurry　　　C．in hurried　　　D．in hurries

（6）Would you please _____ the stain on my shirt?

　　A．move　　　B．remove　　　C．take　　　D．put

（7）I'd like this sweater washed _____ hand _____ cold water.

　　A．in, by　　　B．by, by　　　C．in, in　　　D．by, in

（8）I'll send someone to _____ your laundry.

　　A．pick off　　　B．pick up　　　C．pick down　　　D．pick in

（9）There is something wrong _____ the tap.

　　A．on　　　B．with　　　C．in　　　D．off

（10）The color TV doesn't give the _____ picture.

　　A．clean　　　B．big　　　C．small　　　D．clear

4．翻译句子

（1）我马上派人去取您要洗的衣服。

（2）我可以进来拿走您要洗的衣服吗？

（3）请您重新填写一张洗衣单好吗？

（4）先生，请您查看一下洗好的衣服。

（5）我们可以退还洗衣费。

（6）We will try our best to help you with your laundry.

(7) There is a laundry form in the laundry bag.

(8) May I pick up your laundry?

(9) Please check the items one by one.

(10) Your trousers will be ready in one hour.

任务工单 2　技能操作

工作任务	Laundry Service（洗衣服务）						
姓名		班级		学号		日期	
情境演练	类型：洗衣服务 客人：Mary Smith 房号：Room 2287 洗衣要求：a silk, may fade, by hand, in cold water, sew a button for her husband's jacket 特殊需求：express service, 15% service charge 付款方式：charge to her room						
评估	教师签字：						
自我反思	学生签字：						

学习任务 4　Ordering Room Service（客房订餐服务）

任务工单 1　理论测试

1. 词组互译

（1）美式早餐_____　　（2）七分熟_____

（3）煎蛋_____　　（4）双面煎（蛋黄在上）_____

（5）苏打水_____　　（6）门把手菜单_____

（7）把手推车推走_____　　（8）炸薯条_____

（9）煮蛋（嫩）_____　　（10）黑咖啡_____

（11）Continental breakfast _____　　（12）toast with butter _____

（13）pour the wine _____　　（14）Oriental breakfast _____

（15）green salad _____　　（16）hot cupboard _____

（17）orange juice _____　　（18）over easy _____

（19）sausage and bacon _____　　（20）sign the bill _____

2．根据句意填空（每空一词）

（1）根据上下文填空。

R=Room Service waiter　G=Guest

1）R: Could you care to _____ the bill, please?

　　G: Sure, have you got a pen?

2）R: Shall I _____ the wine?

　　G: Yes, please. But don't pour it.

3）G: What does a Continental breakfast _____ ?

　　R: Chilled orange juice, boiled egg, toast with butter.

4）R: Would you like some tea or _____ , sir?

　　G: Coffee.

5）R: _____ would you like your coffee?

　　G: With milk, please.

（2）根据上下文填空。

W = Waiter　G = Guest

W: Room Service. I've brought you the breakfast, May I come in?

G: Come in, please !

W: Good morning, sir This is your _____. I have one steak sandwich with French fries, one green salad and one glass of soda water, and a bottle of wine. _____ should I put the tray?

G: Thank you. Just put it on the tea table, please.

W: Yes, sir. Shall I _____ it now or shall I leave it _____ the hot cupboard?

G: You can serve it now, I think.

W: Shall I _____ the wine, sir?

G: Yes. please, but don't pour it.

W: There you are, sir. And the plate is very hot, please be careful.

G: Thank you.

W: Would you care to _____ the bill, please?

G: Sure. Have you got a pen, please? Thanks...There you go.

W: Thank you.sir.Would you _____ ringing the Room Service when you finish your meal, sir, and we will take the trolley away? Or if you prefer, you can leave the _____ outside your door.

G: I'll give you a ring and then leave the trolley outside, OK?

W: Yes, sir. Is there _____ I can do for you, sir?

181

G: _____ , thank you.
W: OK, enjoy your meal, sir. Goodbye.
G: Thank you.Goodbye.

3．翻译句子

（1）一天24小时都提供客房送餐服务。

（2）客房送餐服务要加15%的服务费。

（3）您点的牛排要怎样做呢？

（4）先生，我把您订的餐送来了，我可以进来吗？

（5）麻烦您把账单签一下好吗？

任务工单2　技能操作

工作任务	Ordering Room Service（客房订餐服务）						
姓名		班级		学号		日期	
情境演练	类型：客房订餐服务 客人：Mr. White 预订信息：Chilled orange juice, sweet dumpling, soybean milk 房号：Room 2586 要求：问客人想要什么；告知客人room service有10%的service charge						
评估	教师签字：						
自我反思	学生签字：						

学习任务5　Delivering Room Service（客房送餐服务）

任务工单1　理论测试

1．词组互译

（1）客房送餐服务 _____　　　　（2）煎蛋 _____

（3）煮蛋 _____　　　　　　　（4）价目表_____

（5）橙汁 _____　　　　　　　（6）green salad _____

（7）minimum charge _____　　（8）French fries _____

（9）black tea _____　　　　　（10）hot cupboard _____

2．单项选择

（1）What's this in the picture? _____.

  A．Doorknob menu　　B．Room card　　C．Business card　　D．New year card

（2）May I _____ your laundry, please?

  A．clean　　　　　B．collect　　　　C．correct　　　　D．wash

（3）A: _____? B: Soft boiled.

  A．What your eggs　　　　　　　　B．How your eggs

  C．How would you like your eggs　　D．What would you like your eggs

（4）We offer three _____ of breakfast.

  A．pieces　　　　　B．types　　　　　C．bars　　　　　D．notes

（5）May I just read that _____ to you sir?

  A．back　　　　　　B．off　　　　　　C．down　　　　　D．up

（6）What does white coffee mean? _____.

  A．Coffee with sugar　　　　　　B．Coffee without milk

  C．Coffee without sugar　　　　　D．Coffee with milk

（7）Thank you _____ calling and hope you have a nice day.

  A．on　　　　　　　B．to　　　　　　　C．for　　　　　　D．in

（8）The room service means the service of _____.

  A．turn-down　　　　　　　　　B．cleaning the room

  C．the room center　　　　　　　D．sending meals to the guest room

（9）The staff in the laundry department are _____ and we also have the _____.

  A．experienced, professional equipment　　B．experience, professional equipment

  C．experience, professional equipment　　　D．experienced, professional equipment

（10）Room service is available _____.

  A．24 hour a day　　B．24 hours a day　　C．24-hour a day　　D．24 hour two day

3. 翻译句子

(1) 先生，我要把托盘（tray）放到哪里？

(2) 先生，客房送餐服务要收 10% 的服务费。

(3) 女士，您的餐点（order）15 分钟内到达。

(4) We will add the cost to your bill. please sign your name and room number here on the bill.

(5) Which breakfast would you prefer, American or Continental?

4. 判断对错

(1) Room service, also called Food Delivery Service. （   ）
(2) Room service section has no relationship（关系）with the F&B department. （   ）
(3) For room service, guests can order their food by telephone in their room. （   ）
(4) Usually, there is no service charge for room service. （   ）
(5) For room service, we should ask the guests their demands（要求 for cooking）. （   ）

任务工单 2　技能操作

工作任务	Delivering Room Service（客房送餐服务）					
姓名		班级		学号		日期
情境演练	类型：客房送餐服务 客人：Mr. White 预订信息：Chilled orange juice, two Chinese breakfast and a continental breakfast, some sweet dumplings 客房服务员：John 房号：Room 2586 要求：1. 两人一组完成客房送餐对话。 2. John 送餐到客人 White 的房间，为客人一一介绍菜品。 3. 告知客人注意事项。 4. 让客人签写账单。 5. 注意服务礼貌、禁忌					
评估	教师签字：					
自我反思	学生签字：					

项目 3　The Food & Beverage（餐饮部）

学习任务 1　Booking a Table（预订餐台服务）

任务工单 1　理论测试

1. 词组互译

（1）空桌_____　　　　（2）包房_____
（3）旺季_____　　　　（4）大厅_____
（5）餐饮部_____　　　（6）预订记录_____
（7）等候名单_____　　（8）宴会预定_____
（9）2人桌_____　　　　（10）recommendation _____
（11）secure your booking _____　（12）arrange _____
（13）reservation clerk _____　　（14）in advance _____

2. 根据句意填空（每空一词）

　　　　R=Reservationist（预订员）　　G=Guest（客人）

（1）请稍等，我来为您查查是否有空位。

　　　Just a moment, please. I'll _____ for you.

（2）您能否换个时间？

　　　Would you like to make a reservation _____ ?

（3）恐怕那个时间的餐位都已经订满了。

　　　I'm afraid _____ for that time.

（4）我们期待下次能为您效劳。

　　　We hope we'll _____ to serve you.

（5）您是喜欢大厅的餐台还是包房呢？

　　　Would you like a table _____ ?

（6）您想要怎么样摆桌子呢？

　　　How would you like us _____ ?

（7）我们会准备好一切。

　　　We'll _____ in advance.

（8）为了确保您的预订，您需要交20美元的押金。

　　　A deposit of US $20 is required to _____ .

（9）您几点光临？

　　　At what time _____ ?

（10）我们只能保留您的餐位到晚上六点。

　　　　We can only _____.

3．单项选择

（1）Which date would that _____ ?

　　　A．being　　　　　B．are　　　　　C．is　　　　　D．be

（2）What does "Master Card" mean?_____.

　　　A．Credit card　　B．Mail　　　　C．Country　　　D．Person's name

（3）We are looking forward to _____ you.

　　　A．serve　　　　　B．service　　　C．serving　　　D．served

（4）The guests can usually pay their hotel bills by all the ways below, except _____.

　　　A．by credit card　B．by Alipay　　C．in cash　　　D．by mail

（5）The word "reserve" equals to _____ in hotel field.

　　　A．serve　　　　　B．book　　　　C．invest　　　　D．settle the bill

（6）A: _____?

　　　B: Yes, I'd like to book a room for my friend, Cray Smith.

　　　A．How are you　B．May I help you　C．Hello　　　D．How do you do

（7）_____ would you like to pay, sir?

　　　A．How　　　　　B．What　　　　C．Which　　　　D．Who

（8）Sorry, we are _____ booked in the period.

　　　A．fully　　　　　B．full　　　　　C．fulling　　　　D．fulled

（9）Among all the room types, which one is the most expensive? _____.

　　　A．Triple room　　B．Business suite　C．Deluxe suite　D．Presidential suite

（10）A: I'd like to make an adjustment of my reservation

　　　　B: Certainly, sir. May I have the date of your _____, please?

　　　　A．reservation　B．departure　　C．flight　　　　D train

4．翻译句子

（1）您想要什么甜品？

（2）请问您有预订吗？

（3）谢谢您的来电，我们期待着您的光临。

（4）先生，您是想在一楼还是二楼用餐？

（5）我们不能保证什么，但是请相信，我们会尽力的。

任务工单 2 技能操作

工作任务	Booking a Table（预订餐台服务）						
姓名		班级		学号		日期	
情境演练	Hanks 先生电话订餐时，被服务员告知晚上 7 点大厅餐位预订已满。这时，作为餐厅服务员，该如何处理？ 要求：以小组为单位总结出服务员的英文应对语句；注意服务礼貌，尽量劝说客人换个时间或到大厅用餐，并在允许下给予一定优惠						
评估	教师签字：						
自我反思	学生签字：						

学习任务 2 Leading the Guest（引客入位服务）

任务工单 1 理论测试

1．单项选择

（1）It should be _____ you in 20 minutes, sir.

　　A．with　　　　　B．in　　　　　C．at　　　　　D．to

（2）How to express "女引位员" in English? _____.

　　A．Host　　　　　B．Waitress　　　C．Waiter　　　D．Hostess

（3）I'd like a table _____ the window.

　　A．in　　　　　　B．on　　　　　C．by　　　　　D．off

（4）We'd like to book a table _____ eight in the main restaurant.

　　A．off　　　　　　B．for　　　　　D．on　　　　　D．by

（5）We've made a reservation of a table _____ the name of Robert.

　　A．under　　　　B．on　　　　　C．by　　　　　D．off

（6）A: _____?

　　B: A table over there.

　　A．How would like to sit　　　　　B．What would you like to sit

    C. Where would you like to sit   D. When would you like to sit

(7) Could you wait _____ until a table is free, please.

    A. a line   B. in line   C. for line   D. lines

(8) A: Welcome to our restaurant, this way please.

    B: _____

    A. Thank you.   B. Yes.   C. No problem.   D. Follow me, please.

(9) _____ a table on the first floor or on the second floor?

    A. Can you   B. Would you   C. Can you like   D. Would you like

(10) We can only _____ your table until 8 o'clock.

    A. keeping   B. keeps   C. keep   D. kept

2. 选词填空

(1) 你们介意分开坐吗？

    Would you mind sitting _____？(A. separately B. separate)

(2) 要不要我给您的孩子拿一把高椅呢？

    Would you like a _____ for your child? (A. high chair B. tall chair)

(3) 您介意和他人同桌吗？

    Would you mind _____ a table? (A. having B. sharing)

(4) 我们正在恭候您的光临

    We are _____ you. (A. waiting B. expecting)

任务工单 2   技能操作

工作任务	Leading the Guest（引客入位服务）						
姓名		班级		学号		日期	
情境演练	学生自编情境，2～3人一组完成英文引客入位服务。 要求：角色扮演，服务程序全面，要有特殊情况处理，每组每个角色不得少于6句，在同学面前展示，学生互评，教师点评						
评估							
						教师签字：	
自我反思							
						学生签字：	

学习任务 3　Serving Chinese Food（中餐服务）

任务工单 1　理论测试

1. 单项选择

（1）The word "cuisine" means _____.

　　A．菜单　　　　　B．菜系　　　　　C．酒水　　　　　D．大堂吧

（2）Sichuan cuisine is _____ and contains chili.

　　A．sour　　　　　B．sweet　　　　　C．hot　　　　　D．salty

（3）It should be _____ you in 20 minutes, sir.

　　A．with　　　　　B．in　　　　　C．at　　　　　D．to

（4）Dinner will be ready _____ half an hour.

　　A．at　　　　　B．in　　　　　C．on　　　　　D．with

（5）"We know little about Chinese food" means _____.

　　A．We know Chinese food well

　　B．We don't know Chinese food

　　C．We like Chinese food

　　D．We hate Chinese food

（6）Chinese food is divided into _____ styles of cuisine.

　　A．six　　　　　B．seven　　　　　C．eight　　　　　D．nine

（7）A: Would you like _____?

　　B: We want some beer.

　　A．some drinks　　B．something to eat　C．something cold　D．something hot

（8）What does Cantonese cuisine mean in Chinese? _____.

　　A．四川菜　　　　B．淮扬菜　　　　C．广东菜　　　　D．鲁菜

（9）Which is right about the Chinese Cuisines? _____

　　A．Cantonese Cuisine is hot and spicy.　　B．Sichuan Cuisine is hot and spicy.

　　C．Shanghai Cuisine is hot and spicy.　　D．Huaiyang Cuisine is hot and spicy.

2. 翻译句子

（1）您喜欢大厅的餐台还是包房呢？

（2）我们很快就安排你们入座。

（3）这道菜色香味俱全。

(4) Which flavor would you prefer, sweet or chili?

(5) It is a well-known delicacy in Chinese Cuisine.

任务工单 2 技能操作

工作任务	Serving Chinese Food（中餐服务）						
姓名		班级		学号		日期	
情境演练	学生自编情境，2～3 人一组完成英文中餐服务。 要求：角色扮演，服务程序全面，要有特殊情况处理，每组每个角色不得少于 6 句，在同学面前展示，学生互评，教师点评						
评估	教师签字：						
自我反思	学生签字：						

学习任务 4　Serving Western Food（西餐服务）

任务工单 1　理论测试

1．词组互译

（1）主菜 _____　　　　　　（2）热菜 _____

（3）一副刀叉 _____　　　　（4）干白 _____

（5）on the house _____　　 （6）medium well _____

（7）hot pot _____　　　　　（8）take order _____

（9）T-bone steak _____　　 （10）seat guest _____

2．填空

（1）A: Have you got a reservation in our restaurant?

　　　B: Yes. I have a reservation _____（以……的名字）Green.

（2）A: I'm sorry. The tables by the window are all _____（满座了）.

　　　B: Well, it doesn't matter.

（3）A: How would you like the steak?

　　　B: _____（五分熟）.

（4）A: would you like something to drink?

B: Yes, _____（一杯水）, please.

（5）A: Sorry, we do not have _____（蘑菇汤）today.

B: What about tomato soup?

3．单项选择

（1）The correct order of western food is _____.

A．starter – soup – main course – side dish – dessert

B．starter – soup – side dish–main course – dessert

C．dessert – starter – soup – main course – side dish

D．soup – starter – main course –side dish – dessert

（2）_____ would you like your steak?

A．How　　　　B．What　　　　C．Why　　　　D．Which

（3）It is very delicious and worth a _____.

A．look　　　　B．try　　　　C．eating　　　　D．suggestion

任务工单 2　技能操作

工作任务	Serving Western Food（西餐服务）					
姓名		班级		学号		日期
情境演练	学生自编情境，2～3 人一组完成英文西餐服务。 要求：角色扮演，服务程序全面，要有特殊情况处理，每组每个角色不得少于 6 句，在同学面前展示，教生互评，教师点评					
评估	 　 　 教师签字：					
自我反思	 　 　 学生签字：					

学习任务 5　Bar Service（酒吧服务）

任务工单 1　理论测试

1．词组翻译

（1）酒单_____　　　　（2）鸡尾酒_____

（3）酒水_____　　　　（4）点酒水_____

（5）一杯葡萄酒＿＿＿＿＿＿ 　　（6）（酒）烈的＿＿＿＿＿＿

（7）苏打水＿＿＿＿＿＿ 　　　　（8）加冰＿＿＿＿＿＿

（9）伏特加＿＿＿＿＿＿ 　　　　（10）软饮＿＿＿＿＿＿

2．补全对话

对话 1：

H: Is there anything I can do for you?

G: Yes, we'd like to pick up the ＿＿＿＿＿.

H: Sure, ＿＿＿＿＿ a minute, please. (after a while, the waiter came back) Sir, it ＿＿＿＿＿ RMB 480 Yuan.

G: Ok. Here is 500.

H: Here is your ＿＿＿＿＿.

G: You can keep it as tips.

H: Thank you, but we don't accept ＿＿＿＿＿.

G: Ok. Fine. Anyway, thank you for your service.

H: It's my ＿＿＿＿＿. Have a nice day.

对话 2：

A: What can I get ＿＿＿＿＿ you?

B: I'd prefer a brandy.

A: How do you ＿＿＿＿＿ your brandy? Straight ＿＿＿＿＿ or on the rocks?

B: With ice, thank you.

A: Do you want some snacks ＿＿＿＿＿ the drink?

B: What snacks do you sell?

A: We have peanuts and potato chips. But the popcorn is free tonight.

B: OK, give me some popcorn.

任务工单 2　技能操作

工作任务	Bar Service（酒吧服务）						
姓名		班级		学号		日期	
情境演练	学生自编情境，2～3 人一组完成英文酒吧服务。 要求：角色扮演，服务程序全面，要有特殊情况处理，每组每个角色不得少于 6 句，在同学面前展示，学生互评，教师点评						
评估	 教师签字：						
自我反思	 学生签字：						

学习任务 6　Paying the Bill（餐厅结账服务）

任务工单 1　理论测试

1. 翻译单词

（1）fry _____　　　　　　（2）deep fry _____
（3）stir-fry _____　　　　　（4）bake _____
（5）boil _____　　　　　　（6）stew _____
（7）steam _____　　　　　（8）grill _____
（9）smoke _____　　　　　（10）braise _____

2. 单项选择

（1）The word "miscalculation" refers to _____.
　　A．确认　　　　B．算账　　　　C．结账　　　　D．算错账
（2）A: How much is it?
　　B: It comes _____ 300 Yuan, sir.
　　A．to　　　　　B．on　　　　　C．in　　　　　D．up
（3）Let me break it _____ for you, 200 Yuan for food, 300 Yuan for drinks and 10% for service charge.
　　A．up　　　　　B．down　　　　C．to　　　　　D．on
（4）A: What credit card are you _____ , sir?
　　B: VISA card.
　　A．hold　　　　B．holds　　　　C．holding　　　D．held
（5）May I _____ an imprint of your card, please?
　　A．put　　　　B．hit　　　　　C．take　　　　D．reserve
（6）A: _____?
　　B: Yes, sir. Just a moment. Here it is, your bill.
　　A．Can I have the seat　　　　　B．Can I have the table
　　C．Can I have the receipt　　　　D．Can I have the bill
（7）How much is that _____ US dollars.
　　A．in　　　　　B．on　　　　　C．to　　　　　D．up
（8）I _____ got enough cash with me. I wonder if you accept traveler's checks.
　　A．have　　　　B．have not　　　C．do　　　　　D．do not
（9）"Your bill comes to 1 000 Yuan" equals to _____.
　　A．Your bill totals to 1 000 Yuan
　　B．Your bill totals in 1 000 Yuan

C. Your bill totals 1 000 Yuan

D. Your bill totals up 1 000 Yuan

(10) Would you like to _____ this _____ your room?

    A. charge, in   B. charge, to   C. change, in   D. change, to

(11) How to express "我们不收外币" in English? _____

    A. We don't have foreign currency.

    B. We don't want foreign currency.

    C. We don't need foreign currency.

    D. We don't accept foreign currency.

3．填空

(1) Let me go through the _____ with you.（账单）

(2) How do you charge for the _____.（饮料）

(3) I'd like to _____ with Master Card.（付账）

(4) Keep the _____ for you.（零钱）

(5) _____ bill or separate bill, sir?（合单）

(6) Thank you for your _____.（理解）

(7) Sorry, we don't accept _____.（小费）

(8) I'd like two _____ of red wine.（瓶）

(9) Are you in Beijing on _____?（假期）

(10) Is it _____ outside?（热）

4．翻译句子

(1) 我来给您逐项解释一下。

(2) 对不起，我们不收外币。

(3) 请把您的卡拿来刷一下，好吗？

(4) 我们不收小费，谢谢您。

(5) 请在这里签名，好吗？

任务工单 2　技能操作

工作任务	Paying the Bill（餐厅结账服务）						
姓名		班级		学号		日期	
情境演练	学生自编情境，2～3 人一组完成英文餐厅结账服务。 要求：角色扮演，服务程序全面，要有特殊情况处理，每组每个角色不得少于 6 句，在同学面前展示，学生互评，教师点评						
评估	教师签字：						
自我反思	学生签字：						

学习任务 7　Handling Complaints（处理投诉）

任务工单 1　理论测试

1．单项选择

（1）The bathroom isn't clean._____

　　A．Well, I wasn't supposed to clean it.

　　B．I'm terribly sorry about that, ma'am. We'll clean it right away.

（2）Someone else baggage is in my room._____

　　A．Oh, sorry, but I don't know whose baggage it is.

　　B．I'm sorry, sir. I'll see to it immediately.

（3）It's already noon, but no one has come to clean my room yet._____

　　A．I'm sorry, sir. I'll send a room attendant to clean the room for you right away.

　　B．What? Wait a minute, please. Hey, housekeeping? What's the matter with you? Go and clean the room at once.

（4）I am checking out. This place is too noisy. I won't stay here another night. Get my bill ready!_____

　　A．We do apologize for this on behalf of our hotel. Please allow me to offer you another room. I can guarantee it will be very quiet.

　　B．Oh, well, you should have said that earlier.

（5）The carpet（地毯）in my room has a bad odor（气味）._____

195

A. We're awfully sorry, ma'am. We'll send someone to your room right away.

B. That's strange. I've worked here for two years. No one else ever complained about the carpet.

2. 判断对错

（1）Show your sympathy. (　　)

（2）Apologize to the guest. (　　)

（3）Patiently listen to what the guest says and take notes. (　　)

（4）Talk more loudly than the customer. (　　)

（5）Offer one or more solutions to the guest. (　　)

（6）Use the polite service language. (　　)

（7）Tell the guest what will be done at once. (　　)

（8）Tell the guest when the problem will be solved. (　　)

（9）Tell the relevant hotel employees to solve the problem at once. (　　)

（10）Say nothing and continue serving. (　　)

（11）Suggest what the customer is complaining about is not very important. (　　)

（12）Call a senior staff member (e.g. the manager), if you feel that you cannot deal with the problem. (　　)

（13）Remain calm and don't lose your temper. Apologize for each problem. (　　)

（14）Be prepared for what the guest is going to say by reading the information opposite first. (　　)

（15）Try to imply that the guest is at fault, not the staff. (　　)

（16）Treat the complaint as a joke. (　　)

任务工单 2　技能操作

工作任务	Handling Complaints（处理投诉）					
姓名		班级		学号		日期
情境演练	你知道换房时客人的期盼吗？与同桌讨论，并与下列情形做比较，然后说出你们的答案。 1. 我期待酒店换房处理得既便利又专业。 2. 我不希望我换房的请求被酒店员工认为是给他们添麻烦。 3. 我希望酒店能按照我的请求和喜好给我换房。 4. 我希望酒店能快速、友好地处理我换房的请求，为我服务的员工既有职业能力又有职业素养。 5. 我希望所有的物品能够完好地被转移到新房间					
评估	教师签字：					
自我反思	学生签字：					

项目 4　The Fitness Center（康乐部）

学习任务 1　Gym Service（健身房服务）

任务工单 1　理论测试

1．词组翻译

（1）私人教练 _____　　（2）运动设施 _____
（3）最先进的 _____　　（4）热身运动 _____
（5）瑜伽 _____　　（6）武术 _____
（7）更衣室 _____　　（8）贵重物品保存服务 _____
（9）运动衣 _____　　（10）星级水准 _____

2．补全对话

T=Tony Goldfield　　L=Alice Lee

L: Good morning! I'm Alice Lee, the manager of the Recreation & Fitness Center. _____ I help you?

T: Yes. I'm Tony Goldfield. I'm a _____（常驻）guest in your hotel. I've heard that your hotel has one of the best gyms in the city.

L: We're really proud of our Center, Mr. Goldfield. It's really catching on.

T: Do you accept foreign residents for _____ ?

L: Yes. Our membership includes foreign residents as well as visitors.

T: Could you tell me something _____ your facilities?

L: Yes, of course. Please _____ this way and I will _____ you around. We have a very well-equipped _____（健身房）with all the latest fitness apparatus, such as treadmill, stationary bikes, muscle builder sets and everything you need to work out for good physical condition.

T: That's great.

L: Besides, we also have a billiards room and a bowling room. Here is the swimming _____. All the _____（会员）can use the pool any time between 6:00 a.m. and 9:00 p.m.

L: It's really a nice swimming pool. Do you have any traditional _____ exercise like Tai Chi and Qigong?

L: Yes. We have a room specially designed for Tai Chi and Qigong. Mr. Zhang is our resident instructor, who is one of the best instructors in the city.

T: Good. I'm interested in Tai Chi and Qigong.

任务工单 2　技能操作

工作任务	Gym Service（健身房服务）						
姓名		班级		学号		日期	
情境演练	学生自编情境，2～3人一组完成健身房服务。 要求：角色扮演，服务程序全面，要有特殊情况处理，每组每个角色不得少于6句，在同学面前展示，学生互评，教师点评						
评估	 教师签字：						
自我反思	 学生签字：						

学习任务 2　Swimming and Bowling Service（泳池及保龄球服务）

任务工单 1　理论测试

1．词组翻译

（1）resident guest ＿＿＿＿＿＿　　　　（2）resident instructor ＿＿＿＿＿＿

（3）swimming pool ＿＿＿＿＿＿　　　　（4）application form ＿＿＿＿＿＿

（5）keep-fit gym ＿＿＿＿＿＿　　　　　（6）ball lanes ＿＿＿＿＿＿

（7）billiard room ＿＿＿＿＿＿　　　　　（8）bowling service ＿＿＿＿＿＿

（9）warm up exercise ＿＿＿＿＿＿　　　（10）apply for membership ＿＿＿＿＿＿

2．补全对话

Z=Gray Liu　　A=Attendant

A: Good afternoon, sir. ＿＿＿＿＿＿ to our bowling room. Can I help you?

Z: Could you tell me something about your services here?

A: Certainly, sir. There are four ball-lanes in our bowling room. The service hour is from 9:00 a.m. to 12:00 p.m.，and we ＿＿＿＿＿＿ 30 Yuan for one game.

Z: There are many regulations about the bowling service in America. What are yours?

A: Well, ＿＿＿＿＿＿, no vest and no slippers, and drunkards are not allowed. Secondly, special bowling shoes are required, which are available in the bowling room. Thirdly, no food, no drink and no smoking.

Z: I see. We don't have a reservation. Are there any vacant lanes at present?

A: Just a _____ , sir. I'll have to check. (After a while) Thank you for _____ . Yes, sir. There is one. It's the fourth lane. Your _____ size, please.

Z: We are both 40.

A: Here you are. How many games would you like to play? Is it necessary to enter your names on the video screen?

Z: Four games, please. Enter our names, Gray, G-R-A-Y and Wang Hong.

A: Very well, sir. Four games, Gray and Wang Hong. Am I _____ ?

Z: Yes, exactly. Then where shall we pay the _____ , shall we pay it here?

A: Since you are staying at our hotel you may _____ the bill. The hotel will charge you when you leave.

Z: Thank you.

A: I'm _____ your service. Please enjoy yourselves. If there's anything else you need, let us know.

Z: Thank you. No problem.

任务工单 2 技能操作

工作任务	Swimming and Bowling Service（泳池及保龄球服务）					
姓名		班级		学号		日期
情境演练	学生自编情境，2～3人一组完成泳池及保龄球服务。 要求：角色扮演，服务程序全面，要有特殊情况处理，每组每个角色不得少于6句，在同学面前展示，学生互评，教师点评					
评估	教师签字：					
自我反思	学生签字：					

项目 5　The Business Center（商务中心）

学习任务 1　Booking Tickets（票务服务）

任务工单 1　理论测试

1. 词组翻译

（1）经济舱 _____　　（2）卧铺 _____

（3）直达航班 _____　　（4）非吸烟区 _____

（5）头等舱 _____　　（6）过道 _____

（7）软卧 _____　　（8）（票）卖完 _____

（9）单程票 _____　　（10）往返票 _____

2. 补全对话

H: Hello, Sir! What can I do for you?

L: I want to _____（预订）a train-ticket of hard sleeping berth from Beijing to Chongqing — _____ Feb.1st.

H: Yes! Let me have check. There are two trains leaving for Chongqing on that day, one is _____（快车），and the other is ordinary. What kind of trains do you prefer?

L: The express train is the best.

H: Mr. Smith, the booking office said that there are two trains only on the 2nd and 3rd in February until now. Do you like to book?

L: I'd like to book a train on the 2nd.

H: Please pay 500 Yuan RMB _____（预先）; I'll _____（结账）the account with you after we have got the ticket.

L: Ok. Thank you!

H: Good bye, Mr. Hanks! Have a pleasant day.

任务工单 2 技能操作

工作任务	Booking Tickets（票务服务）					
姓名		班级		学号		日期
情境演练	酒店工作人员为 Hanks 先生订购的机票因故没有预订上，现在要告诉他并建议采用其他方式订票。 要求：角色扮演，服务程序全面，要有特殊情况处理，每组每个角色不得少于 6 句，在同学面前展示，学生互评，教师点评					
评估	 教师签字：					
自我反思	 学生签字：					

学习任务 2　Secretarial Service（文秘服务）

任务工单 1　理论测试

1．词组翻译

（1）复印 _____　　（2）打字 _____

（3）原件 _____　　（4）装订 _____

（5）放大 _____　　（6）出故障 _____

（7）服务费 _____　　（8）病毒 _____

（9）最低收费 _____　　（10）发传真 _____

2．补全对话

L: Good Morning, Mr. Smith! What can I do for you?

H: Hello! I'd like to have the material _____（打印）.

L: No problem. When do you want it?

H: Before noon today.

L: Do you have any _____（特殊的）demands?

H: No, thanks.

L: When do I send the first draft to you for proofreading after I finish typing?

H: About 10: 00 a.m.

L: Where do I send to?

H: Please send them to the meeting room _____ (直接地).

L: That's good. I'll do it _____ (尽可能快地).

H: That's good. Thank you. See you!

L: See you!

L: Could you _____ (签字) your name here?

H: Sure!

任务工单 2 技能操作

工作任务	Secretarial Service（文秘服务）						
姓名		班级		学号		日期	
情境演练	学生自编情境，2～3人一组完成英文文件处理服务。 要求：角色扮演，服务程序全面，要有特殊情况处理，每组每个角色不得少于6句，在同学面前展示，学生互评，教师点评						
评估	 教师签字：						
自我反思	 学生签字：						